SONGS OF CHALLENGE

SONGS OF CHALLENGE
An anthology selected and arranged
by ROBERT FROTHINGHAM

HOUGHTON MIFFLIN COMPANY
THE RIVERSIDE PRESS CAMBRIDGE
1922

The Riverside Press
CAMBRIDGE · MASSACHUSETTS
PRINTED IN THE U.S.A

TO

ERMAN J. RIDGWAY

"Yet always the aspiring Soul, —
The Angel in the mortal clod,
The Vision that defies control, —
Will look through Nature up to God;
And strive in word and form to speak
The beauty it was born to seek."

FOREWORD

Man has always been at war with himself, and every now and again he awakens to the consciousness that his discontent is divine. Then he turns in weariness from his greatest material accomplishments toward the "Happy Isles" of his imagination. We all have our secret dreams, which generally include a revolt against our own limitations and a longing for better things than those we know.

"Whence" and "Whither" will ever be inseparable phases of the Great Adventure, as the real man views it. And, inasmuch as this compilation is meant for that particular breed, it will be quite apparent to him that there is no intent to "point a moral or adorn a tale," to either affirm or deny, and least of all, to constitute itself a moral or spiritual finger-board.

From the standpoint of the materialist, one of life's tragedies lies in the fact that so many of us know so many things that are n't so. Scarce one of us, however, but recognizes that

> "When the fight begins within himself,
> A man's worth something."

Pin us down and you'll find that most of us believe in our kinship with the worth-while things, the truly big things, "the stars which fleck our journey's dusks." But it's like squaring the circle when we try to weave that belief into the warp and woof of our daily grind. The great majority of us are essentially religious — not theologically nor doctrinally, and frequently not even intellectually. But — in the inner recesses of our spirit, where joy works alone, there is a glow like unto the fire of a mountain sunset of which the most wondrous view is to be had from the most distant range: our soul's intimate dream, human nature's Holy of Holies. Here, under an impulse, conscious or unconscious, to be free of laws and restraints, with the thousand and one superfluous precepts of poor, timorous humanity thrown aside, without the necessity for breaking our shins against the Decalogue or rubbing our shoulders raw under the yoke of any particular creed, we kneel to "whatever gods may be" and strive to play the game.

Of all the lessons brought home to us by the World War, this reawakening of our relationship with the Unseen, with its consequent reëstablishment of spiritual values is, perhaps, the most significant. We needed to be reminded of the fact that man pays. He has always paid: for being born, for living, for dying. The principal thing that has distinguished us from our early ancestors is that we have been trying to get too much for our money. We have been taking out more than we put in. We invited a crash and we got it. Praises be, however, along with it has come the Vision that is helping a lot of us off the treadmill: the Vision of the Spirit of Song. When a man can sing acceptably about either his belief or his unbelief, whether it agrees with what you and I think or not, we can afford to stop and listen; in fact, we can't afford not to do so.

Some writer has said that human needs are the true ligatures between God and man. How small vanities disappear and how vital stout sincerity becomes in the face of such a belief!

· · ·

There are a lot of men who claim to have no liking for poetry, others who read it surreptitiously as though it were forbidden fruit, and still others who profess to regard a love for it as a sort of effeminate dilettantism. The very word "poetry" conveys a wrong meaning to some men. This little book is filled with robust verse, intended to appeal to the very men I have described. If it has any mission at all, it seeks simply to make vivid that Vision which pierces the murk and scatters our up-to-date cocksureness to the four winds, and to restore to hearts grown callous and dour the inspiration and the warmth of the Spirit of Song:

"Beholding dimly from afar the glory of the Hidden
    Face —
Our worship ever our reward, the quest our golden
    coronal."

                                        R. F.

New York
October, 1922

ACKNOWLEDGMENTS

The editor acknowledges his indebtedness to the following authors and publishers for the use of copyright poems:

Messrs. Angus & Robertson, Ltd., Sydney, Australia, for "Only Laughter is Sure," from *The Australian*, and "Stars in the Mist," from *Hearts of Gold*, by Will H. Ogilvie; and "He Giveth his Beloved Sleep," from *Rio Grande's Last Race*, by Major A. B. Paterson.

Mr. Richard G. Badger for "A Cowboy's Prayer," from *Sun and Saddle Leather*, by Badger Clark.

The Bookfellows of Chicago for "Requiem" and "The Great Adventure," from *Phantom Caravans*, by Major Kendall Banning.

Messrs. Chappell & Co., music publishers, London, and the author for "Hush your Prayers," by Conal O'Riordon (Norreys Connell, *pseud.*)

Messrs. Dodd, Mead & Co. for "Nirvana," from *Poems*, by Rosamund Marriott Watson; and "He fell among Thieves," from *The Island Race*, by Sir Henry Newbolt.

Messrs. George H. Doran Company for "A Poet Enlists," from *The Silver Trumpet* (copyright, 1918), and "Because I Have Loved Life," from *Life and Living* (copyright, 1916), by Amelia Josephine Burr.

Messrs. Doubleday, Page & Co. for "The Awakening," from *Poems and Portraits*, by Don Marquis;

and "Darest thou now, O Soul," "Passage to India," and "Song of the Universal," from *Leaves of Grass,* by Walt Whitman.

Messrs. Duffield & Co. for "Wine of Omar Khayyám," from *Mimma Bella,* by Eugene Lee-Hamilton.

Messrs. E. P. Dutton & Co. for permission to publish "The Dance of Death," from *The Collected Poems* of Austin Dobson.

Messrs. Forbes & Co. for "The Certain Victory," from *Ballads of the Busy Days,* by S. E. Kiser.

The Franklin Press for "He whom a Dream hath Possessed," from *The Blossomy Bough,* by Shaemas O'Sheel.

Messrs. Harper & Brothers for "The Seeker," from *Dreams and Dust,* by Don Marquis; and "At the Top of the Road," from *Star-Glow and Song,* by Charles Buxton Going.

Messrs. Houghton Mifflin Company for "Make me no Grave" and "The Sun-Worshipers," from *Songs of the Trail,* by Henry Herbert Knibbs; "Waiting," by John Burroughs; "Live your Life, then take your Hat," by Henry David Thoreau; "The Problem," by Ralph Waldo Emerson; "Dawn in the Desert," from *Poems,* by Clinton Scollard; "Io Victis," by William Wetmore Story; and "Room for a Soldier," by Thomas William Parsons.

Mr. Richard LeGallienne for "The Second Crucifixion."

Messrs. Little, Brown & Co. for "Coronation," from *Poems,* by Helen Hunt Jackson.

Erskine Macdonald for "Courage," by the late Lieut. Dyneley Hussey.

The Macmillan Company for "Atoms and Ages" and "Peace on Earth," from *Collected Poems* by Edwin Arlington Robinson; and "April Theology," "Prayer for Pain," and "When I have gone Weird Ways," from *The Quest,* by John G. Neihardt.

Mr. Thomas Bird Mosher for "Tears," from *A Wayside Lute,* by Lizette Woodworth Reese; and "A Man's Bargain," from *Tomorrow's Road,* by Gertrude M. Hort.

Messrs. G. P. Putnam's Sons for "Each in his Own Tongue," from *Each in his Own Tongue, and Other Poems,* by William Herbert Carruth; and "The Washerwoman's Song" and "Kriterion," from *Rhymes of Ironquill,* by Eugene F. Ware.

George Routledge & Sons for "The Dance of Death," from *The Collected Poems* of Austin Dobson.

Mr. Porter E. Sargent for "A Man's Guess" and "The Question," from *Miscellaneous Moods,* by Elihu Vedder.

Messrs. Charles Scribner's Sons for "Atoms and Ages," from *Children of the Night,* by Edwin Arlington Robinson; and "The Departed Friend" and "If this were Faith," by Robert Louis Stevenson.

Messrs. Small, Maynard & Co. for "The Lost Comrade," "Fear not the Menace," and "Sceptics," from *Last Songs from Vagabondia,* by Richard Hovey and Bliss Carman.

Messrs. Smith, Elder & Co. for "Before Action," from *Verse and Prose in Peace and War,* by the late Lieut. W. N. Hodgson.

Messrs. P. F. Volland & Co. for "Each in his Own Tongue," by William Herbert Carruth.

Yale University Press for "Hunger," from *Shadow Verses*, by Gamaliel Bradford; and "The Dying Pantheist to the Priest," from *Poems*, by Henry A. Beers.

The American-Scandinavian Foundation for "Longing," by Viktor Rydberg; and "Prayer amid Flames," by Verner von Heidenstam, from *Anthology of Swedish Lyrics*.

Century Magazine for "When the Time for Parting Comes," by Dorothea Lawrance Mann.

Chicago Tribune for "A Nation's Face Upturned," by John Bemer Crosby.

Contemporary Verse for "The Naturalist on a June Sunday," by Leonora Speyer; "Make no Desperate Search for God," by John French Wilson; and "One Path," by William Alexander Percy.

McClure's Magazine for "The Pipes o' Gordon's Men," by J. Scott Glasgow.

The Nation for "The Pagan," by Rose Henderson.

New York Sun for "Prayer of a Poet to God," by Joseph Bernard Rethy.

New York Times for "The Laughing Prayer," by Louise Driscoll; and "Deferred," by Stokely S. Fisher.

New York Tribune for "The Last Tourney," "Dissolution," "Worship," "Litany," and "To Captain Dale Mabry," by Frederic F. Van de Water; and "When Charon Beckons," by Francis Woolsey Bronson.

The Outlook for "I Accept," by Harold Trowbridge Pulsifer.

Reedy's Mirror for "Exile from God," by John Hall Wheelock.

The Roycrofters Anthology for "The Agnostic's Creed," by Walter Malone.

Saturday Evening Post for "With the Tide," by Edith Wharton.

CONTENTS

CONTENTS

SONGS OF CHALLENGE

I ACCEPT

I shall go out as all men go,
Spent flickers in a mighty wind,
Then I shall know as all must know,
What lies the great gray veil behind.

There may be nothing but a deep
And timeless void without a name
Where no sun hangs, no dead stars sleep,
And there is neither night nor flame.

There may be meadows there and hills,
Mountains and plains and winds that blow,
And flowers bending over rills
Springing from an eternal snow.

There may be oceans white with foam
And great tall ships for hungry men
Who called our little salt seas home,
And burn to launch their keels again.

There may be voices I have known,
Cool fingers that have touched my hair;
There may be hearts that were my own —
Love may abide forever there.

Who knows? Who needs to understand
If there be shadows there, or more —

To live as though a pleasant land
Lay just beyond an open door?
Harold Trowbridge Pulsifer

HUSH YOUR PRAYERS

Hush your prayers — 't is no saintly soul
Comes fainting back from the foughten field;
Carry me forth on my broken shield;
Trumpet and drum shall my requiem yield —
Silence the bells that toll.

Dig no hole in the ground for me:
Though my body be made of mould and must,
Ne'er in the earth shall my dead bones rust;
Give my corse to the flame's white lust,
And sink my ashes at sea.

Reeking still with the sweat of the strife,
Never a prayer have I to say,
(My lips long since have forgotten the way)
Save this: "I have sorrowed sore in my day —
But I thank Thee, God, for my life."
Norreys Connell

PRAYER FOR PAIN

I do not pray for peace nor ease,
Nor truce from sorrow:
No suppliant on servile knees
Begs here against to-morrow!

Lean flame against lean flame we flash,
O Fates that meet me fair;

Blue steel against blue steel we clash —
Lay on, and I shall dare!

But Thou of deeps the awful Deep,
Thou breather in the clay,
Grant this my only prayer — Oh keep
My soul from turning gray!

For until now, whatever wrought
Against my sweet desires,
My days were smitten harps strung taut,
My nights were slumbrous lyres.

And howsoe'er the hard blow rang
Upon my battered shield,
Some lark-like, soaring spirit sang
Above my battle-field;

And through my soul of stormy night
The zigzag blue-flame ran.
I asked no odds — I fought my fight —
Events against a man.

But now — at last — the gray mist chokes
And numbs me. Leave me pain!
Oh let me feel the biting strokes
That I may fight again!

John G. Neihardt

A MAN'S BARGAIN

If I cry out for fellowship,
A comrade's voice, a comrade's grip,
A hand to hold me when I slip,
    An ear to heed my groan —

Renew that dark hour's ecstasy!
When all Thy waves went over me,
And Thou and I, with none to see,
    Were joined in fight alone.

If I demand a sheltered space
Set for me in the battle-place,
Where I at times could turn my face,
    A screened and welcomed guest, —
Decree my soul should henceforth cease
From its wild hankering after peace,
And rest in that which gives release
    From the desire for rest.

If I for final goal should ask —
Some meaning for the long day's task,
Some ripened field that yet may bask,
    Secure from hurricane, —
Point to Thy locust-eaten sheaves —
The burnt-out stars, the still-born leaves!
And by the Toil no hope retrieves
    Nerve me to toil again.

So, to Thy hard, propitious skies
Shall praise go up like sacrifice,
And all the will within me rise,
    Applauding at Thy word:
Thou, in the Glory, jasper-walled,
By no reproach of mine be galled:
And I, among my kind, be called
    The man whose prayers are heard.

G. M. Hort

THE LAST TOURNEY

I shall go forth one day to joust with death;
The brittle little chains that hold me tied
To rusted hopes, to visions cracked and dried,
Shall break, and I shall hear the trumpet's breath
Go clamoring across the barren heath,
And for a flaming moment I shall ride
The lists' brief course to meet the Undefied —
And take the blow that I shall fall beneath.

Each day I make this single fervent prayer:
May then the blood of Bayard be my own;
May I ride hard and straight and smite him square,
And in a clash of arms be overthrown;
And as I fall hear through the evening air
The distant horn of Roland, faintly blown.

Frederic F. Van de Water

WHEN CHARON BECKONS

When Charon beckons me and marks my place
Within his barge, where whimpering souls are
      pressed
So close together that the damned and blessed
Seem one vague lump of blasphemy and grace;
When fearlessly my eyes explore that space
Called Heaven or Hell by some, by others Rest,
I 'll mock the gasps of every awe-struck guest
And turn toward that shore a tranquil face.

For when that hour comes, as come it will,
My lips shall rim the cup of life to quaff

The bitter-sweetish dregs — I shall not spill
　　One solitary drop — and then I 'll laugh
And lilt a sonnet with my dying breath
And cram a quatrain 'twixt the teeth of Death.
　　　　　　　　　　Francis Woolsey Bronson

ONE FIGHT MORE

Fear death? — to feel the fog in my throat,
　　The mist in my face,
When the snows begin, and the blasts denote
　　I am nearing the place,
The power of the night, the press of the storm,
　　The post of the foe;
Where he stands, the Arch Fear in a visible form,
　　Yet the strong man must go:
For the journey is done and the summit attain'd,
　　And the barriers fall,
Though a battle's to fight ere the guerdon be gain'd,
　　The reward of it all.
I was ever a fighter, so — one fight more,
　　The best and the last!
I would hate that death bandaged my eyes, and for-
　　　　bore,
　　And bade me creep past.
No! let me taste the whole of it, fare like my peers
　　The heroes of old,
Bear the brunt, in a minute pay glad life's arrears
　　Of pain, darkness and cold.
For sudden the worst turns the best to the brave,
　　The black minute 's at end,
And the elements' rage, the fiend-voices that rave,
　　Shall dwindle, shall blend,

Shall change, shall become first a peace out of pain.
   Then a light, then thy breast,
O thou soul of my soul! I shall clasp thee again,
   And with God be the rest!

Robert Browning

BEFORE ACTION

By all the glories of the day,
And the cool evening's benison:
By the last sunset touch that lay
Upon the hills when day was done:
By beauty lavishly outpoured,
And blessings carelessly received,
By all the days that I have lived —
Make me a soldier, Lord.

By all of all men's hopes and fears,
And all the wonders poets sing,
The laughter of unclouded years,
And every sad and lovely thing:
By the romantic ages stored
With high endeavour that was his,
By all his mad catastrophes —
Make me a man, O Lord.

I, that on my familiar hill
Saw with uncomprehending eyes
A hundred of Thy sunsets spill
Their fresh and sanguine sacrifice,
Ere the sun swings his noonday sword
Must say good-bye to all of this: —
By all delights that I shall miss —
Help me to die, O Lord.

Lieut. W. N. Hodgson

"DIE, DRIVEN AGAINST THE WALL"

A man said unto his Angel:
"My spirits are fallen low,
And I cannot carry this battle:
O brother! where might I go?

"The terrible Kings are on me
With spears that are deadly bright;
Against me so from the cradle
Do fate and my fathers fight."

Then said to the man his Angel:
"Thou wavering, witless soul,
Back to the ranks! What matter
To win or to lose the whole,

"As judged by the little judges
Who hearken not well, nor see?
Not thus, by the outer issue,
The Wise shall interpret thee.

"Thy will is the sovereign measure
And only event of things:
The puniest heart, defying,
Were stronger than all these Kings.

"Though out of the past they gather,
Mind's Doubt and Bodily Pain,
And pallid Thirst of the Spirit
That is kin to the other twain,

"And Grief, in a cloud of banners,
And ringletted Vain Desires,

And Vice with the spoils upon him
Of thee and thy beaten sires, —

"While Kings of eternal evil
Yet darken the hills about,
Thy part is with broken saber
To rise on the last redoubt;

"To fear not sensible failure,
Nor covet the game at all,
But fighting, fighting, fighting,
Die, driven against the wall!"

Louise Imogen Guiney

LONGING

He longs with a tireless yearning,
Still seeking, wandering, turning
At all times and everywhere,
The sought-for goal receding,
Flitting, enticing, leading
With shifting likeness fair.

A nodding flower of azure
Above the field's ripe treasure
First lures the wanderer on;
But when he would stoop to pick it,
It sinks in the billowy thicket
Of rye-blades and is gone.

A banner all golden-rifted,
That spirit hands have lifted,

On sunset towers upborne,
An echo resounding faintly
That's blown from an old and quaintly-
Wrought silver legend-horn.

An organ-rapture outpouring
From some great cathedral soaring
'Mid streets where visions dwell;
The blow of a hammer thund'rous
When angels rear a wondrous
Dream-lovely citadel.

A sighing of ocean surges
When dawn's first wave emerges
On night's pale galaxy, —
He listens and looks with yearning,
Still this way and that way turning
To find what it may be.

A sea to which years run lightly,
A river that mirrors brightly
The Spring and its beauties rare,
Beside whose waters haunted
Two mortals languish enchanted
And see but each other there.

The river hastes from the flowers
To Autumn's golden bowers,
And whirls the dry leaves they wore
To Ocean, the dark Unbounded,
The wanderer staring astounded,
Asks: "What of the farther shore?"

Perhaps his desire is bended
On something uncomprehended,
Which no man may comprehend;
But he must ever be yearning,
Must ever be wandering, turning,
And seeking it without end.

And should he reach World's Ending,
With no road further tending,
The border of Nothingness, —
He'd bend him over the steep there
And gaze into the deep there
With straining-eyed distress.

And leaning over the steep there,
He'd cry into the deep there, —
That echoless, vast Untrod, —
And onward the shout should go where
Is naught but the void of Nowhere,
Go ringing through Chaos: "God!"

From the Swedish of Viktor Rydberg
Translated by Charles Wharton Stork

THE COLLAR

I struck the board, and cried, "No more;
    I will abroad.
What! shall I ever sigh and pine?
My lines and life are free; free as the road,
    Loose as the wind, as large as store.
        Shall I be still in suit?
Have I no harvest but a thorn
To let me blood and not restore
What I have lost with cordial fruit?

"Sure there was wine,
Before my sighs did dry it; there was corn
Before my tears did drown it;
Is the year only lost to me?
Have I no bays to crown it,
No flowers, no garlands gay? all blasted,
All wasted?
Not so, my heart; but there is fruit,
And thou hast hands.

"Recover all thy sigh-blown age
On double pleasures; leave thy cold dispute
Of what is fit and not; forsake thy cage,
Thy rope of sands
Which petty thoughts have made; and made to
thee
Good cable, to enforce and draw,
And be thy law,
While thou didst wink and wouldst not see.

"Away! take heed;
I will abroad.
Call in thy death's-head there, tie up thy fears;
He that forbears
To suit and serve his need
Deserves his load."
But as I raved and grew more fierce and wild
At every word,
Methought I heard one calling, "Child!"
And I replied, "My Lord!"

George Herbert

MAKE ME NO GRAVE

Make me no grave within that quiet place
   Where friends shall sadly view the grassy mound,
Politely solemn for a little space,
   As though the spirit slept beneath the ground.

For me no sorrow, nor the hopeless tear;
   No chant, no prayer, no tender eulogy:
I may be laughing with the gods — while here
   You weep alone. Then make no grave for me.

But lay me where the pines, austere and tall,
   Sing in the wind that sweeps across the West:
Where night, imperious, sets her coronal
   Of silver stars upon the mountain crest.

Where dawn, rejoicing, rises from the deep,
   And Life, rejoicing, rises with the dawn:
Mark not the spot upon the sunny steep,
   For with the morning light I shall be gone.

Far trails await me; valleys vast and still,
   Vistas undreamed-of, cañon-guarded streams,
Lowland and range, fair meadow, flower-girt hill,
   Forests enchanted, filled with magic dreams.

And I shall find brave comrades on the way:
   None shall be lonely in adventuring,
For each a chosen task to round the day,
   New glories to amaze, new songs to sing.

Loud swells the wind along the mountain-side,
   High burns the sun, unfettered swings the sea,

Clear gleam the trails whereon the vanished ride,
  Life calls to life: then make no grave for me!
                    Henry Herbert Knibbs

REQUIEM

When I am dead, pray me no prayers;
  Intone no mummer's rhyme,
Nor let the surpliced gentry ply
  Their priestly pantomime.
Return, O God, my errant flesh
  Back to my mother earth,
Wherein my dust may serve again, —
  — God will, at Spring's rebirth.
Send back my dreams unto the hills
  Whence, on the winds, they came;
Let strong, my passions, seek their own —
  Flame back to quivering flame!
Into Thy hands return that love
  Men call the soul of me —
And give my spirit back to the indomitable sea.
                    Major Kendall Banning

A NATION'S FACE UPTURNED

October 4, 1914

The leader of our nation bids us pray;
He bids us pray that alien wars shall cease;
    He bids us pray
    All on one day —
To pray, the mass of all of us — for peace.

We're not a praying nation, in the main;
We list, in mass, toward shallow-rooted dare;

And yet his words
Have moved our herds
Of bold and cynic hearts to pristine prayer!

No race are we — yet race of races made;
Careless, impatient, and each day rebrained;
And still the core
Of our heart has more
Of reverence than ever yet has drained.

We are not skilled in prayer — nor know the form
That shall befit the crisis of our kin
Where'er they bide;
And yet he cried
Not vainly; for we sense the smell of sin;

And though we do not pray to sate the code,
We pray in euphony of honest hearts;
Our stumbling word
Will yet be heard
Above the rattle of the armored carts.

For know we that a prayer is but a wish
From heart so deep that rhetoric's poor plumb
Falls short, bereft
Of use; but left —
God finds the music of the hope born dumb.

In the tongue of every sufferer shall we pray —
With bungled, mumbled language hesitant;
But more 't will mean
On God to lean
With such than with the best the poets grant.

And some will name the god they seek,
And some will limn his face!
And some will scar his thought of them
By hedging 'round his place;
And some will fear the god they speak,
And some will say "My Brother —"
And some will say "My Father dear —"
And some, this, that or other;
And every kind of god they hail
Will smile, and take their message,
And carry it to the God of gods —
You see what small things presage?

As a fleck of dust on an ocean crest
From the deck of a scoured yacht
Will look this earth, minute, of ours
To the God of gods as He turns His face,
'Mid the woven swirls of all His worlds,
In the whir of His frozen space —

And yet will He heed; and He will say,
"What do my people wish to-day?
What is their debt they cannot pay?
Let mine own ear discern the hum
Of their discord: I bid them come."

And then, obscure as a gnat at night,
Shall we tell THE GOD of our brothers' plight:

And this our blurted prayer: —

"Fools they may be to fools have named
As masters of men — whose rule has maimed

The bravest they had of muscle and soul —
    Yet we forgive their folly!

"They have exalted as Lords of Earth
The helmets small, and the wide of girth —
They took the road and they've paid the toll —
    And there's no rebate on folly.

"And now the mesh they have woven well
Is snaring them and their kin to hell.
For setting the spear above the poll —
    Lord God, condone their folly!

"We speak not of ourselves at all,
Lest we seek to exalt ourselves — and fall;
'T would not be true if we should state
    That we alone know Thee.

"But, seeing our brothers in shrapnel hail —
Stung by the pang of their children's wail —
Scenting the skunk at the palace gate —
    We fear they have forgotten; —

"Our brothers are drunk with the taste of blood,
Their brains are sprayed with the sanguine flood —
Impregnate them with a hate for hate —
    We pray Thee, Lord!

"Teach Thou them to love but Love —
Guide their baffled brains above —
Turn their hands to the worthy wheat —
    For their sake, Lord!

"Map for the kings their ending path —
Touch their tongues in Thy cup of wrath —
Flash in their eyes the judgment seat
    For the kings' souls' sake, O Lord!

"'Lords of War' look very small;
Bid Thou them act not at all —
Bid Thou them reject the pall —
Bid Thou them avert the fall
By acceptance of Thy call —
    We pray Thee, Lord!

"And if our hopes be not too great —
And since Thou'rt kind enough to wait
For us to speak our plea devout —
    (We thank Thee, Lord!) —

"Let us ask, for ourselves alone,
A word of cheer, to still our moan —
We mean so well — but so much doubt
    What is Thy will —

"We feel so sure Thou soon wilt curb —
From Teuton lord to humble Serb,
From Saxon hull to Slavic knout —
    Thy flouting, Lord.

"That it is hard for us to be
As patient as Thou think'st that we
(In view of our exempted lives,
    Mayhap), should bide:

"Dear Lord, the gods of our sects have failed;
Facing their frowns no monarch quailed;

Our gods all tried to do the right —
Our gods all sought to stop the fight,
    But lacked the might;

"So now They come with us to THEE —
Our gods and us, on doubled knee —
Seeking to bathe in Thy great light,
    O, God of gods!

"And thus we pray to Thee, Lord God —
Craving Thy love — nor fearing Thy rod —
    Daring to face Thee from our hives —
    We, our children and our wives —
    Craving Thy deservèd gyves —
    Placing in Thy hands our lives —

"We pray Thee, Lord,
To guide us in our baffling days —
Stay us in our swaying ways —
Answer as our hearts have cried —
    Stop these wars!
    Oh, Lord of Peace!"
          John Bemer Crosby

A COWBOY'S PRAYER

O Lord, I've never lived where churches grow.
    I love creation better as it stood
That day You finished it so long ago
    And looked upon your work and called it good.
I know that others find You in the light
    That's sifted down through tinted window-panes.
And yet I seem to feel You near to-night
    In this dim, quiet starlight on the plains.

I thank You, Lord, that I am placed so well,
  That You have made my freedom so complete;
That I'm no slave of whistle, clock or bell,
  Nor weak-eyed prisoner of wall and street.
Just let me live my life as I've begun
  And give me work that's open to the sky;
Make me a pardner of the wind and sun,
  And I won't ask a life that's soft or high.

Let me be easy on the man that's down;
  Let me be square and generous with all.
I'm careless sometimes, Lord, when I'm in town,
  But never let 'em say I'm mean or small!
Make me as big and open as the plains,
  As honest as the hawse between my knees,
Clean as the wind that blows behind the rains,
  Free as the hawk that circles down the breeze.

Forgive me, Lord, if sometimes I forget.
  You know about the reasons that are hid.
You understand the things that gall and fret;
  You know me better than my mother did.
Just keep an eye on all that's done and said
  And right me, sometimes, when I turn aside,
And guide me on the long, dim trail ahead
  That stretches upward toward the Great Divide.

Badger Clark

"BECAUSE I HAVE LOVED LIFE"

Because I have loved life, I shall have no sorrow to
  die.
I have sent up my gladness on wings, to be lost in
  the blue of the sky.

I have run and leaped with the rain, I have taken
the wind to my breast.
My cheek like a drowsy child to the face of the
earth I have pressed.

Because I have loved life, I shall have no sorrow to
die.
I have kissed young Love on the lips, I have heard
his song to the end.
I have struck my hand like a seal in the loyal hand
of a friend.
I have known the peace of heaven, the comfort of
work done well.
I have longed for death in the darkness and risen
alive out of hell.

Because I have loved life, I shall have no sorrow to
die.
I give a share of my soul to the world where my
course is run.
I know that another shall finish the task I must
leave undone.
I know that no flower, no flint was in vain on the
path I trod.
As one looks on a face through a window, through
life I have looked on God.
Because I have loved life, I shall have no sorrow to
die.

Amelia Josephine Burr

HE FELL AMONG THIEVES

"Ye have robb'd," said he, "ye have slaughter'd
    and made an end;
  Take your ill-got plunder, and bury the dead:
What will ye more of your guest and sometime
    friend?"
    "Blood for our blood," *they said*.

He laugh'd: "If *one* may settle the score for five,
  I am ready; but let the reckoning stand till
    day:
I have loved the sunlight as dearly as any alive."
    "You shall die at dawn," *said they*.

He flung his empty revolver down the slope,
  He climb'd alone to the Eastward edge of the
    trees;
All night long in a dream untroubled of hope
  He brooded, clasping his knees.

He did not hear the monotonous roar that fills
  The ravine where the Yassin river sullenly flows;
He did not see the starlight on the Laspur hills,
  Or the far Afghan snows.

He saw the April noon on his books aglow,
  The wistaria trailing in at the window wide;
He heard his father's voice from the terrace below
  Calling him down to ride.

He saw the gray little church across the park,
  The mounds that hid the loved and honour'd
    dead;

The Norman arch, the chancel softly dark,
   The brasses black and red.

He saw the School-close, sunny and green,
   The runner beside him, the stand by the para-
      pet wall,
The distant tape, and the crowd roaring between,
   His own name over all.

He saw the dark wainscot and timber'd roof,
   The long tables, and the faces merry and keen;
The College Eight and their trainer dining aloof,
   The Dons on the dais serene.

He watch'd the liner's stem ploughing the foam,
   He felt her trembling speed and the thrash of
      her screw;
He heard the passengers' voices talking of home,
   He saw the flag she flew.

And now it was dawn. He rose strong on his
      feet,
   And strode to his ruin'd camp below the wood;
He drank the breath of the morning cool and
      sweet:
   His murderers round him stood.

Light on the Laspur hills was broadening fast,
   The blood-red snow-peaks chill'd to a dazzling
      white;
He turn'd, and saw the golden circle at last,
   Cut by the Eastern height.

"O glorious Life, Who dwellest in earth and sun:
 I have lived, I praise and adore Thee."

                                        A sword swept.
Over the pass the voices one by one
 Faded, and the hill slept.

                              Sir Henry Newbolt

PEACE ON EARTH

He took a frayed hat from his head,
And "Peace on Earth" was what he said.
"A morsel out of what you're worth,
And there we have it: Peace on Earth.
Not much, although a little more
Than what there was on earth before.
I'm as you see, I'm Ichabod, —
But never mind the ways I've trod;
I'm sober now, so help me God!"

I could not pass the fellow by:
"Do you believe in God?" said I;
"And is there to be Peace on Earth?"

"To-night we celebrate the birth,"
He said, "of One who died for men;
The Son of God, we say. What then?
Your God, or mine? I'd make you laugh
Were I to tell you even half
That I have learned of mine to-day
Where yours would hardly seem to stay.
Could He but follow in and out
Some anthropoids I know about,
The god to whom you may have prayed
Might see a world He never made."

"Your words are flowing full," said I;
"But yet they give me no reply;
Your fountain might as well be dry."

"A wiser One than you, my friend,
Would wait and hear me to the end;
And for his eyes a light would shine
Through this unpleasant shell of mine
That in your fancy makes of me
A Christmas curiosity.
All right, I might be worse than that;
And you might now be lying flat;
I might have done it from behind,
And taken what there was to find.
Don't worry, for I 'm not that kind.
'Do I believe in God?' Is that
The price to-night of a new hat?
Has he commanded that his name
Be written everywhere the same?
Have all who live in every place
Identified his hidden face?
Who knows but he may like as well
My story as one you may tell?
And if he show me there be Peace
On Earth, as there be fields and trees
Outside a jail-yard, am I wrong
If now I sing him a new song?
Your world is in yourself, my friend,
For your endurance to the end;
And all the Peace there is on Earth
Is faith in what your world is worth,
And saying, without any lies,
Your world could not be otherwise."

"One might say that and then be shot,"
I told him; and he said: "Why not?"
I ceased, and gave him rather more
Than he was counting of my store.

"And since I have it, thanks to you,
Don't ask me what I mean to do,"
Said he: "Believe that even I
Would rather tell the truth than lie —
On Christmas Eve. No matter why."

His unshaved, educated face,
His inextinguishable grace,
And his hard smile, are with me still,
Deplore the vision as I will;
For whatsoever he be at,
So droll a derelict as that
Should have at least another hat.
                              Edwin Arlington Robinson

WORSHIP

I think that God might hear my prayer,
If I could kneel and worship where
A simple folk on Sunday use
The shallow ranks of narrow pews
As seats that audience afford
Before an almost-visioned Lord.
If I might see them kneeling, dressed
In strait and awkward Sabbath best,
To celebrate His ordained day,
I almost might relearn to pray.

I'd like to watch his careful tread
Along the aisle, red-carpeted;
His white bow-tie, his rusty frock —
Old shepherd of a failing flock,
Who all the years his way has trod,
One hand upon the arm of God;
To see him in the pulpit stand,
And beat the time with withered hand,
And smile upon us as we raise
Old Hundred's ancient hymn of praise.

Perhaps his stark theology
Would fan to flame no spark in me.
I wonder if, to hail the Throne,
One needs a sanctimonious tone,
And must each plea for aid propose
In words that issue through the nose?
I doubt if heaven greatly savors
Hymns quite so full of flats and quavers;
But yet, perhaps, they rise far higher
Than anthems of a vested choir.

But I have watched the sunlight come,
Across the long prayer's drone and hum,
To touch a crown of thin, white hair
And weave a golden halo there;
Have seen, through windows open wide,
Broad fields where bobolinks abide;
Have seen the grasses sway and glisten
And daisies bow their heads to listen
Beneath a tranquil summer sky —
And heard God's footsteps passing by.

                    Frederic F. Van de Water

NAUGHTY NELL

There came a knock at the door of Heaven
And the knock was firm and light.
St. Peter he opened the window grill
And looked on a puzzling sight:
A maiden sweet as a swaying bough
Of apple-buds pink and white.

He scratched his forehead and looked again:
No doubt but the girl was fair,
She lowered the lids of her blue-bell eyes
With a half impenitent air,
And the smile that lurked in her pouting lips
Had little to do with prayer.

"Name?" he inquired in formal tones.
"Nell Bassett," the answer fell.
"If you please, I thought I might come and knock
Before I was dragged to hell,
Though there's small use looking my record up,
For my nickname was Naughty Nell."

St. Peter he stretched to a dusty shelf
And hefted a volume down,
He read in the light that the halo shed
From the bald rim of his crown:
"Ah! Bassett, Eleanor, nineteen-two,
June twentieth, Dorking town."

He scanned her over the edge of the book,
And she answered him, "Yes, that's I.
I've never done anything good, I know,
But I didn't have long to try.

I'd always meant to begin some day
Before I came to die."

"That's odd, for I find you lost your life
In the fever that came this year
Nursing a child whose mother died
While the rest kept away in fear."
"You would n't have had me let it starve,
The poor little lonely dear!"

"You were the girl that fought Bill Jenks
When he came home drunk one night,
And his wife screamed 'Help!' but never a man
Durst enter the house for fright."
"Why, who was gladder of that than Bill
Next day when his head was right?"

"Be still, please, Nell. — Your case is clear,
Your faults are but light and few;
Here's a page and a half of kindly deeds
That your short life found to do.
I need not hold you a minute more
From the bliss that waits for you."

The door swung wide, and a sudden glow
Of radiance blossomed out,
The air was rich with the scent of myrrh,
With song and triumphal shout;
Yet over the face of the dazzled girl
Came a look as of fear and doubt.

"Please, but it's all a mistake, I'm feared,"
She stammered; "I was n't good.

I always did what I chose to do
As often as ever I could,
I never moidered and vexed myself
The way I was told I should.

"Are you sure that all of my sins are down, —
The time that I ran away
From prayers with Ned into Folsom Wood
And tarried there all the day,
And he kissed my lips that kissed again
By the streamside as we lay?"

"Whatever was sin is entered here,"
Said Peter, and smote his book,
For his temper was short, the worthy saint.
But when he had cast a look
At the trouble that shadowed the girl's clear eyes,
All anger his heart forsook.

"Please help me," she faltered. "I know it's
          wrong,
But I feel a bit naughty still.
I want to frolic and race and dance,
Not sit and do God's will;
Will there anybody like me be there,
Or is everyone staid and chill?"

Then Peter laughed — he could do no less —
"Why, Nell, are you then afraid
That Heaven will be like Dorking town
At church or dress parade,
That tongues are still and thoughts are chill —
And everyone dull and staid?

"The beams of light that spread on earth,
When your clean spirit shone,
Were darted from the crystal depth
Of the Eternal Throne.
Hark to the rapturous shouts of praise
To Him Who sits thereon!

"The golden voice of sympathy,
The gallant din of mirth
That lust and pride and selfish fear
Have deafened upon earth,
All wishes flowering beauty-wards
That drooped of old in dearth —

"All these win free as purest thought
To flame aloft in heaven,
All oppositions melt away,
The rusted chains are riven,
A vast unending festival
To joy, to joy is given!"

His ancient, youthful voice was still,
Too weak to utter more,
And Naughty Nell bowed silently
To marvel and adore;
Then, calm with ecstasy, she rose
And passed through the shining door.

                              Charles Wharton Stork

CORONATION

At the king's gate the subtle noon
   Wove filmy yellow nets of sun;
Into the drowsy snare too soon
   The guards fell one by one.

Through the king's gate, unquestioned then,
   A beggar went, and laughed: "This brings
Me chance, at last, to see if men
   Fare better, being kings."

The king sat bowed beneath his crown,
   Propping his face with listless hand;
Watching the hour-glass sifting down —
   Too slow its shining sand.

"Poor man, what wouldst thou have of me?"—
   The beggar turned, and pitying,
Replied, like one in dream, "Of thee,
   Nothing. I want the king."

Uprose the king, and from his head
   Shook off the crown, and threw it by —
"O man, thou must have known," he said,
   "A greater king than I."

Through all the gates, unquestioned then,
   Went king and beggar hand in hand.
Whispered the king, "Shall I know when
   Before His throne I stand?"

The beggar laughed. Free winds in haste
   Were wiping from the king's hot brow

The crimson lines the crown had traced —
  "This is his presence, now."

At the king's gate, the crafty noon
  Unwove its yellow nets of sun;
Out of their sleep in terror soon
  The guards waked one by one.

"Ho here! Ho there! Has no man seen
  The king?" The cry ran to and fro;
Beggar and king, they laughed, I ween,
  The laugh that free men know.

On the king's gate the moss grew gray;
  The king came not. They called him dead;
And made his eldest son one day
  Slave in his father's stead.

                  Helen Hunt Jackson

A POET ENLISTS

And all the songs that I might sing —
  Madness to risk them so, you say?
How is it such a certain thing
  That I can sing them if I stay?

The winds of God are past control,
  They answer to no human call,
And if I lose my living soul
  That is — for me — the end of all.

Better to shout one last great song,
  Dying myself, to dying men,

Than crawl the bitter years along
And never sing again.
                        Amelia Josephine Burr

VASTNESS

Many a hearth upon our dark globe sighs after
    many a vanish'd face,
Many a planet by many a sun may roll with the
    dust of a vanish'd race.

Raving politics, never at rest — as this poor earth's
    pale history runs, —
What is it all but a trouble of ants in the gleam of a
    million million of suns?

Lies upon this side, lies upon that side, truthless
    violence mourn'd by the Wise,
Thousands of voices drowning his own in a popular
    torrent of lies upon lies;

Stately purposes, valor in battle, glorious annals of
    army and fleet,
Death for the right cause, death for the wrong
    cause, trumpets of victory, groans of defeat;

Innocence seeth'd in her mother's milk, and Char-
    ity setting the martyr aflame;
Thraldom who walks with the banner of Freedom,
    and recks not to ruin a realm in her name;

Faith at her zenith, or all but lost in the gloom of
    doubts that darken the schools;
Craft with a bunch of all-heal in her hand, follow'd
    up by her vassal legion of fools;

Trade flying over a thousand seas with her spice
and her vintage, her silk and her corn;
Desolate offing, sailorless harbors, famishing popu-
lace, wharves forlorn;

Star of the morning, Hope in the sunrise; gloom of
the evening, Life at a close;
Pleasure who flaunts on her wide downway with
her flying robe and her poison'd rose;

Pain, that has crawl'd from the corpse of Pleasure,
a worm which writhes all day, and at night
Stirs up again in the heart of the sleeper, and stings
him back to the curse of the light;

Wealth with his wines and his wedded harlots;
honest Poverty, bare to the bone;
Opulent Avarice, lean as Poverty; Flattery gilding
the rift in a throne;

Fame blowing out from her golden trumpet a jubilant challenge to Time and to Fate;
Slander, her shadow, sowing the nettle on all the
laurell'd graves of the Great;

Love for the maiden, crown'd with marriage, no re-
grets for aught that has been,
Household, happiness, gracious children, debtless
competence, golden mean;

National hatreds of whole generations, and pigmy
spites of the village spire;
Vows that will last to the last death-ruckle, and
vows that are snapp'd in a moment of fire;

He that has liv'd for the lust of a minute, and died
    in the doing it, flesh without mind;
He that has nail'd all flesh to the Cross, till Self
    died out in the love of his kind;

Spring and Summer and Autumn and Winter, and
    all these old revolutions of earth;
All new-old revolutions of Empire — change of the
    tide — what is all of it worth?

What the philosophies, all the sciences, poesy,
    varying voices of prayer?
All that is noblest, all that is basest, all that is filthy
    with all that is fair?

What is it all, if we all of us end but in being our
    own corpse-coffins at last,
Swallow'd in Vastness, lost in Silence, drown'd in
    the deeps of a meaningless Past?

What but a murmur of gnats in the gloom, or a mo-
    ment's anger of bees in their hive? —
.   .   .   .

Peace, let it be! for I loved him, and love him for
    ever: the dead are not dead — but alive.
                  Tennyson

"THE WORLD IS TOO MUCH WITH US"

The world is too much with us; late and soon,
Getting and spending, we lay waste our powers:
Little we see in Nature that is ours.
          Great God! I'd rather be
A Pagan suckled in a creed outworn;

So might I standing on this pleasant lea,
Have glimpses that would make me less forlorn;
Have sight of Proteus rising from the sea;
Or hear old Triton blow his wreathèd horn.

Wordsworth

EARTH GETS ITS PRICE

Earth gets its price for what Earth gives us;
   The beggar is taxed for a corner to die in,
The priest hath his fee who comes and shrives us,
   We bargain for the graves we lie in;
At the devil's booth are all things sold,
Each ounce of dross costs its ounce of gold;
   For a cap and bells our lives we pay,
Bubbles we buy with a whole soul's tasking:
   'T is heaven alone that is given away,
'T is only God may be had for the asking;
No price is set on the lavish summer;
June may be had by the poorest comer.

James Russell Lowell

THE LIE

   Go, Soul, the Body's guest,
      Upon a thankless arrant;
   Fear not to touch the best;
      The truth shall be thy warrant:
   Go, since I needs must die,
   And give the World the lie.

   Say to the Court, it glows
      And shines like rotten wood:

Say to the Church, it shows
    What's good, and doth no good:
If Court and Church reply
Then give them both the lie.

Tell Potentates, they live
    Acting by others' action,
Not loved unless they give,
    Not strong but by a faction:
If Potentates reply,
Give Potentates the lie.

Tell men of high condition
    That manage the Estate,
Their purpose is ambition,
    Their practice, only hate:
And if they once reply,
Then give them all the lie.

Tell them that brave it most,
    They beg for more by spending,
Who, in their greatest cost,
    Seek nothing but commending:
And if they make reply,
Then give them all the lie.

Tell Zeal it wants devotion;
    Tell Love it is but lust;
Tell Time it is but motion;
    Tell Flesh it is but dust:
And wish them not reply,
For thou must give the lie.

Tell Age it daily wasteth;
  Tell Honor how it alters;
Tell Beauty how she blasteth;
  Tell Favor how it falters:
And as they shall reply,
Give every one the lie.

Tell Wit how much it wrangles
  In tickle points of niceness;
Tell Wisdom she entangles
  Herself in over-wiseness:
And when they do reply,
Straight give them both the lie.

Tell Physic of her boldness;
  Tell Skill it is pretension;
Tell Charity of coldness;
  Tell Law it is contention:
And as they do reply,
So give them still the lie.

Tell Fortune of her blindness;
  Tell Nature of decay;
Tell Friendship of unkindness;
  Tell Justice of delay:
And if they will reply,
Then give them all the lie.

Tell Arts they have no soundness,
  But vary by esteeming;
Tell Schools they want profoundness,
  And stand too much on seeming:
If Arts and Schools reply,
Give Arts and Schools the lie.

Tell Faith it's fled the City;
    Tell how the Country erreth,
Tell Manhood shakes off pity;
    Tell Virtue least preferreth:
And if they do reply,
Spare not to give the lie.

So when thou hast, as I
    Commanded thee, done blabbing,
Although to give the lie
    Deserves no less than stabbing, —
Yet, stab at thee that will,
No stab the soul can kill!

                              Sir Walter Raleigh

LITANY

Give me Thy grace;
Not for the shouting assault when my banner advances;
Not for the thunder of hooves and the tempest of
    lances.
Keep Thou my face
Calm in the heart-breaking crash of the overturned
    dream.
When to my mouth comes the sickening, salt taste
    of fear,
And over the tumult and cries of the vanquished I
    hear
The hurrying wings of the Furies; their hideous
    scream —
Give me Thy steadfastness then, O God. Give me
    Thy grace!

Give me Thy mirth;

Not for the sun and the sky and the summer wind's
laughter,

Not for the meeting of friends and the wine that
flows after.

But when the earth

Hardens to iron and the winds of adversity blow,

When the past walks, a terrible ghost, and the future is vain, —

Give me Thy bright gift of laughter to flaunt before
pain;

Give me Thy smile to fling stark in the teeth of the
foe;

Give me the flame of Thy manhood, God. Give me
Thy mirth.

Hear me, O Lord!

Teach me to stand on my feet in the final black
hour;

Turn Thou my eyes unafraid to the oncoming
power.

Give me a sword!

Grant that I cry for no shield to withstand his bleak
blade,

But a hilt in my hand and an edge that the foeman
may feel;

Let me pass to the chime and the chant and the
clangor of steel,

That You see and rejoice in the soul of the man You
have made;

This is my prayer to You, God of Men. Hear me, O
Lord!

Frederic F. Van de Water

THE LOST COMRADE

Now who will tell me aright
The way my lost companion went in the night?
My vanished comrade who passed from the roofs of
      men,
And will not come again.

I have wandered up and down
Through all the streets of this bright and busy town,
Yet no one has seen a trace of him since the day
He silently went away.

I have haunted the wharves and the slips,
And talked with foreigners from the incoming
      ships,
But when I questioned them closely about my
      friend,
They seemed not to comprehend.

From men of book-learning, too,
I have sought knowledge, confident that they knew,
But when I inquired simply about my chum,
They glanced at me and were dumb.

I have entered your churches of stone,
And heard discourse about God and the throng
      'round his throne,
But the preacher knew nothing at all, when I broke
      in with: "Where?" —
And the people could only stare.

Ah, no, you may read and read,
Pile modern heresy upon ancient creed!

But for all your study you know no more than I,
Under the open sky.

So — 't is, Back to the Inn for me,
Where my great friend and I were happy and free.
And I will remember his beautiful words and his
      ways,
For the rest of my days;

How eager he was for truth,
Yet never scorned the good things of his youth —
The soul of gentleness and the soul of love!
I shall be wise enough.

               Bliss Carman

"I SHALL NOT SCORN MY GRAVE"

Let me at last be laid
On that hillside I know which scans the vale,
Beneath the thick yews' shade,
For shelter when the rains and winds prevail.
It cannot be the eye
Is blinded when we die,
So that we know no more at all
The dawn's increase, the evening's fall;
Shut up within a mouldering chest of wood
Asleep, and careless of our children's good.

Shall I not feel the spring,
The yearly resurrection of the earth,
Stir thro' each sleeping thing
With the fair throbbings and alarms of birth,
Calling at its own hour
On folded leaf and flower,

Calling the lamb, the lark, the bee,
Calling the crocus and anemone,
Calling new lustre to the maiden's eye,
And to the youth love and ambition high?

Shall I no more admire
The winding river kiss the daisied plain?
Nor see the dawn's cold fire .
Steal downward from the rosy hills again?
Nor watch the frowning cloud,
Sublime with mutterings loud,
Burst on the vale, nor eves of gold,
Nor crescent moons, nor starlights cold,
Nor the red casements glimmer on the hill
At Yule-tides, when the frozen leas are still?

Or, should my children's tread
Through Sabbath twilights, when the hymns are
        done,
Come swiftly overhead,
Shall no sweet quickening through my bosom run,
Till all my soul exhale
Into the primrose pale,
And every flower which springs above
Breathes a new perfume from my love;
And I shall throb, and stir, and thrill beneath,
With a pure passion stronger far than death?

Sweet thought! fair, gracious dream,
Too fair and fleeting for our clearer view!
How should our reason deem
That those dear souls, who sleep beneath the blue,

In rayless caverns dim,
'Mid ocean monsters grim,
Or whitening on the trackless sand,
Or with strange corpses on each hand
In battle-trench or city graveyard lie,
Break not their prison-bonds till time shall die?

Nay, 't is not so indeed:
With the last fluttering of the falling breath
The clay-cold form doth breed
A viewless essence, far too fine for death;
And, ere one voice can mourn,
On upward pinions borne,
They are hidden, they are hidden, in some thin air,
Far from corruption, far from care,
Where through a veil they view their former scene,
Only a little touch'd by what has been.

Touch'd but a little; and yet,
Conscious of every change that doth befall,
By constant change beset,
The creatures of this tiny whirling ball,
Fill'd with a higher being,
Dower'd with a clearer seeing,
Risen to a vaster scheme of life,
To wider joys and nobler strife,
Viewing our little human hopes and fears
As we our children's fleeting smiles and tears.

Then, whether with fire they burn
This dwelling-house of mine when I am fled,
And in a marble urn
My ashes rest by my belovèd dead,

Or in the sweet cold earth
I pass from death to birth,
And pay kind Nature's life-long debt
In heart's-ease and in violet —
In charnel-yard or hidden ocean wave,
Where'er I lie, I shall not scorn my grave.

Sir Lewis Morris

WAITING

Serene, I fold my hands and wait,
   Nor care for wind, or tide, or sea;
I rave no more 'gainst time or fate,
   For, lo! my own shall come to me.

I stay my haste, I make delays,
   For what avails this eager pace?
I stand amid the eternal ways,
   And what is mine shall know my face.

Asleep, awake, by night or day,
   The friends I seek are seeking me;
No wind can drive my bark astray,
   Nor change the tide of destiny.

What matter if I stand alone?
   I wait with joy the coming years;
My heart shall reap where it has sown,
   And garner up its fruit of tears.

The waters know their own and draw
   The brook that springs in yonder height;
So flows the good with equal law
   Unto the soul of pure delight.

The stars come nightly to the sky;
    The tidal wave unto the sea;
Nor time, nor space, nor deep, nor high,
    Can keep my own away from me.

John Burroughs

WHAT IS TO COME

What is to come we know not. But we know
That what has been was good — was good to show,
Better to hide, and best of all to bear.
We are the masters of the days that were:
We have lived, we have loved, we have suffered
    ... even so.

Shall we not take the ebb who had the flow?
Life was our friend. Now, if it be our foe —
E'en though it spoil and break us! — need we care
    What is to come?

Let the great winds their worst and wildest blow,
Or the gold weather round us mellow slow:
We have fulfilled ourselves, and we can dare
And we can conquer, though we may not share
In the rich quiet of the afterglow
    What is to come.

W. E. Henley

THE NATURALIST ON A JUNE SUNDAY

My old gardener leans on his hoe,
Tells me the way that green things grow;
"Goin' to church? Why, no.
All nature's church enough for me!"
Says he.

"Preachin' o' flower and choir o' bird,
An' the wind passin' the plate —
Sweetest service that ever *I* heard,
That's straight!
Eternal Rest?
What for, friend?
Gimme a swarm o' bees to tend,
A honey-makin', world without end,
That's what *I'd* like the best!
(Scoop 'em right up an' find the queen,
They'd not sting *me* — the bees ain't mean!)

"Heaven's all right!
But still I guess I'll kinder miss
The Lady Lunar-moth at night
And the White Wanderer butterfly
Crawlin' out of its chrysalis!
I want my heaven human too,
'Twixt me an' you —
Why, I'd jus' love to see
A chipmunk hop up to the Lord
An' eat right out o' His dread Hand
Same as it does to me!
Eternity! Eternity!
Don't it sound grand?
But say,
What's the matter with to-day?
Just step into the wood an' take a look!
Ain't that a page o' teachin' from the Holy Book?
'He that hath eyes to see
An' ears to hear' —
That's good enough for me!
I guess God's pretty near,

He'll understand, *I* know,
  Why I ain't in no hurry to let June go!"

My old gardener turns to his hoe,
Helping the green things how to grow,
"The Missus can go to church for me!
Amen!" says he.

Leonora Speyer

EACH IN HIS OWN TONGUE

A fire-mist and a planet, —
  A crystal and a cell, —
A jellyfish and a saurian,
  And caves where the cave-men dwell;
Then a sense of law and beauty,
  And a face turned from the clod, —
Some call it Evolution,
  And others call it God.

A haze on the far horizon,
  The infinite, tender sky,
The ripe, rich tint of the cornfields,
  And the wild geese sailing high, —
And all over upland and lowland
  The charm of the goldenrod, —
Some of us call it Autumn,
  And others call it God.

Like tides on a crescent sea-beach,
  When the moon is new and thin,
Into our hearts high yearnings
  Come welling and surging in, —

Come from the mystic ocean,
  Whose rim no foot has trod, —
Some of us call it Longing,
  And others call it God.

A picket frozen on duty, —
  A mother starved for her brood, —
Socrates drinking the hemlock,
  And Jesus on the rood;
And millions who, humble and nameless,
  The straight, hard pathway plod, —
Some call it Consecration,
  And others call it God.

William Herbert Carruth

"AD CŒLUM"

At the Muezzin's Call for prayer,
The kneeling Faithful thronged the square,
And on Pushkara's lofty height
The dark priest chanted Brahma's might.
Amid a monastery's weeds
An old Franciscan told his beads;
While to the synagogue there came
A Jew, to praise Jehovah's name.
The one great God looked down and smiled
And counted each his loving child;
For Turk and Brahmin, monk and Jew
Had reached Him through the gods they knew.

Harry Romaine

HUNGER

I've been a hopeless sinner but I understand a
saint,
Their bend of weary knees and their contortions
long and faint,
And the endless pricks of conscience, like a hundred thousand pins,
A real perpetual penance for imaginary sins.

I love to wander widely but I understand a cell,
Where you tell and tell your beads because you've
nothing else to tell,
Where the crimson joy of flesh, with all its wild,
fantastic tricks,
Is forgotten in the blinding glory of the crucifix.

I cannot speak for others but my inmost soul is
torn
With a battle of desires making all my life forlorn.
There are moments when I would untread the paths
that I have trod.
I'm a haunter of the devil but I hunger after God.

Gamaliel Bradford

LIVE YOUR LIFE — THEN TAKE YOUR HAT

Conscience is instinct bred in the house;
Feeling and Thinking propagate the sin
By an unnatural breeding in and in.
I say, Turn it outdoors,
Into the moors.

I love a life whose plot is simple,
And does not thicken with every pimple,
A soul so sound no sickly conscience binds it,
That makes the universe no worse than 't finds it.
I love an earnest soul
Whose mighty joy and sorrow
Are not drowned in a bowl,
And brought to life to-morrow;
That lives one tragedy,
And not seventy;
A conscience worth keeping,
Laughing, not weeping;
A conscience wise and steady,
And forever ready;
Not changing with events,
Dealing in compliments;
A conscience exercised about
Large things, where one *may* doubt.
I love a soul not all of wood,
Predestinated to be good,
But true to the backbone
Unto itself alone,
And false to none;
Born to its own affairs,
Its own joys and own cares;
By whom the work which God begun
Is finished, and not undone;
Taken up where He left off,
Whether to worship or to scoff;
If not good, why then evil,
If not good god, good devil.
Goodness! — you hypocrite, come out of that,
Live your life, do your work, then take your hat.

I have no patience towards
Such conscientious cowards.
Give me simple laboring folk,
Who love their work,
Whose virtue is a song
To cheer God along.

Henry David Thoreau

THE LAUGHING PRAYER

The sorry prayers go up to God
   Day after weary day,
They whimper through the eternal blue
   And down the Milky Way.

Deaf to the music of the stars,
   The children of desire,
Beggars before the Throne of God,
   They wait for God to tire.

The proletariat of Heaven
   Swarmed in the golden street
One day when Michael's host came by
   Up to the Judgment Seat.

Above the heavenly mansions
   Bright, streaming banners flowed,
While cherubim and seraphim
   Were crowding in the road.

And then a little, laughing prayer
   Came running from the sky,
Along the golden gutters where
   The sorry prayers went by.

It had no fear of anything,
    But in that holy place
It found the very Throne of God
    And smiled up in His face.

Then Michael waited in the road,
    For Michael understood,
While God looked on the laughing prayer
    And found it sweet and good.

So God was comforted. He said:
    "There still is hope for men.
One man prays happily!" And so
    He turned to care again.

Louise Driscoll

THE COAST OF COURAGE

O Mighty Lord of Trade's high-running sea,
    Grant us an echo of that distant main,
    Beyond dark wastes of danger to attain
The Coast of Courage! Strand of Bravery!
Grant an Assurance and a Hope more free
    That over stiller waters we may gain
    At length a vaster vision, not in vain,
Of Thine eternal Opportunity!

Prepare a highway in this wilderness
    Of wanton ways of traffic, a new heart
    Of love and law and Justice in the Mart,
A loftier view of Commerce, limitless,
That sees no end therein Thou would'st not bless,
    No consummation other than Thou art!

Anonymous

UNBELIEF

There is no unbelief;
Whoever plants a seed beneath the sod
And waits to see it push away the clod —
        He trusts in God.

Whoever says when clouds are in the sky:
"Be patient, heart; light breaketh by and by,"
        Trusts the Most High.

Whoever sees 'neath Winter's field of snow
The silent harvest of the future grow,
        God's power must know.

Whoever lies down on his couch to sleep,
Content to lock each sense in slumber deep,
        Knows God will keep.

Whoever says, "To-morrow," "The Unknown,"
"The Future," trusts the Power alone
        He dares disown.

The heart that looks on when eyelids close,
And dares to live when life has woes —
        God's comfort knows.

There is no unbelief;
And day by day, unconsciously,
The heart lives by that faith the lips deny —
        God knoweth why!

                                Owen Meredith

THE LAST CAMP-FIRE

Scar not earth's breast that I may have
Somewhere above her heart a grave;
Mine was a life whose swift desire
Bent ever less to dust than fire;
Then through the swift white path of flame
Send back my soul to whence it came;
From some great peak, storm challenging,
My death-fire to the heavens fling;
The rocks my altar, and above
The still eyes of the stars I love;
No hymn, save as the midnight wind
Comes whispering to seek his kind.

Heap high the logs of spruce and pine,
Balsam for spices and for wine;
Brown cones, and knots a golden blur
Of hoarded pitch, more sweet than myrrh;
Cedar, to stream across the dark
Its scented embers spark on spark;
Long, shaggy boughs of juniper,
And silvery, odorous sheaves of fir;
Spice-wood, to die in incense smoke
Against the stubborn roots of oak,
Red to the last for hate or love
As that red stubborn heart above.

Watch till the last pale ember dies,
Till wan and low the dead pyre lies,
Then let the thin white ashes blow
To all earth's winds a finer snow;

There is no wind of hers but I
Have loved it as it whistled by;
No leaf whose life I would not share,
No weed that is not some way fair;
Hedge not my dust in one close urn,
It is to these I would return,—
The wild, free winds, the things that know
No master's rule, no ordered row,—

To be, if Nature will, at length
Part of some great tree's noble strength;
Growth of the grass; to live anew
In many a wild-flower's richer hue;
Find immortality, indeed,
In ripened heart of fruit and seed.
Time grants not any man redress
Of his broad law, forgetfulness;
I parley not with shaft and stone,
Content that in the perfume blown
From next year's hillsides something sweet
And mine, shall make earth more complete.

Sharlot M. Hall

AFTER DEATH IN ARABIA

He who died at Azan sends
This to comfort all his friends:

Faithful friends! It lies, I know,
Pale and white and cold as snow;
And ye say, "Abdallah's dead!"—
Weeping at the feet and head.

I can see your falling tears,
I can hear your sighs and prayers;
Yet I smile and whisper this,—
"I am not the thing you kiss;
Cease your tears, and let it lie;
It *was* mine, it is not I."

Sweet friends! What the women lave
For its last bed of the grave,
Is a tent which I am quitting,
Is a garment no more fitting,
Is a cage from which, at last,
Like a hawk my soul hath pass'd.
Love the inmate, not the room,—
The wearer, not the garb, — the plume
Of the falcon, not the bars
Which kept him from these splendid stars.

Loving friends! Be wise, and dry
Straightway every weeping eye,—
What ye lift upon the bier
Is not worth a wistful tear.
'T is an empty sea-shell, — one
Out of which the pearl is gone;
The shell is broken, it lies there;
The pearl, the all, the soul, is here.
'T is an earthen jar, whose lid
Allah seal'd, the while it hid
That treasure of his treasury,
A mind that lov'd him; let it lie!
Let the shard be earth's once more,
Since the gold shines in his store!

Allah glorious! Allah good!
Now thy world is understood;
Now the long, long wonder ends;
Yet ye weep, my erring friends,
While the man whom ye call dead,
In unspoken bliss, instead,
Lives and loves you; lost, 't is true,
By such light as shines for you;
But in light ye cannot see
Of unfulfill'd felicity,—
In enlarging paradise,
Lives a life that never dies.

Farewell, friends! Yet not farewell;
Where I am, ye, too, shall dwell.
I am gone before your face,
A moment's time, a little space.
When ye come where I have stepp'd
Ye will wonder why ye wept;
Ye will know, by wise love taught,
That here is all, and there is naught.
Weep awhile, if ye are fain,—
Sunshine still must follow rain;
Only not at death, — for death,
Now I know, is that first breath
Which our souls draw when we enter
Life, which is of all life centre.

Be ye certain all seems love,
View'd from Allah's throne above;
Be ye stout of heart, and come
Bravely onward to your home!

La Allah illa Allah! yea!
Thou love divine! Thou love alway!

He that died at Azan gave
This to those who made his grave.
                              Edwin Arnold

ONLY LAUGHTER IS SURE

Send us Laughter, O gods, for our life is but
    vain;
We are bruised by its rods, we are galled by its
    chain.
What doth patience avail, or the strength to endure
In the fight where we fail? Only Laughter is sure!

Faith is comrade no more. Sorrow sees us and
    nods.
From your generous store give us Laughter, O
    gods;
That with sword of it girt, and with helm of it
    crowned,
We may battle unhurt, we may wander unbound!

Send us Laughter, great lords, for our woes are too
    deep
To be served by the swords save of Laughter or
    Sleep!
Send us Laughter, O gods, and the world is our
    own,
From the cloud to the clods, from the cot to the
    throne!

It shall soften the sting of the whips that are
  whirled,
And a balm it shall bring for the wounds of the
  world.
It shall lighten the rods, it shall cover the sore;
Send us Laughter, O gods, for our armour of war!
         W. H. Ogilvie

MYSTERY

What is this mystery that men call death?
My friend before me lies; in all save breath
He seems the same as yesterday. His face
So like to life, so calm, bears not a trace
Of that great change which all of us so dread.
I gaze on him and say: He is not dead,
But sleeps; and soon he will arise and take
Me by the hand, I know he will awake
And smile on me as he did yesterday;
And he will have some gentle word to say,
Some kindly deed to do; for loving thought
Was warp and woof of which his life was wrought.
He is not dead. Such souls forever live
In boundless measure of the love they give.
         Jerome B. Bell

HYMN OF EMPEDOCLES

 Is it so small a thing
 To have enjoy'd the sun,
 To have lived light in the spring,
 To have loved, to have thought, to have done;
To have advanced true friends, and beat down baf-
  fling foes;

That we must feign a bliss
Of doubtful future date,
And while we dream on this
Lose all our present state,
And relegate to worlds yet distant our repose?

Not much, I know, you prize
What pleasures may be had,
Who look on life with eyes
Estranged, like mine, and sad:
And yet the village churl feels the truth more
    than you;

Who's loth to leave this life
Which to him little yields:
His hard-task'd, sunburnt wife,
His often-labour'd fields;
The boors with whom he talk'd, the country
    spots he knew.

But thou, because thou hear'st
Men scoff at Heaven and Fate;
Because the gods thou fear'st
Fail to make blest thy state,
Tremblest, and wilt not dare to trust the joys
    there are.

I say, fear not! Life still
Leaves human effort scope.
But, since life teems with ill,
Nurse no extravagant hope.
Because thou must not dream thou need'st
    not then despair.

Matthew Arnold

DESERVINGS

This is the height of our deserts:
A little pity for life's hurts;
A little rain, a little sun,
A little sleep when work is done.

A little righteous punishment,
Less for our deeds than their intent;
A little pardon now and then,
Because we are but struggling men.

A little light to show the way,
A little guidance where we stray;
A little love before we pass
To rest beneath the kirkyard grass.

A little faith, in days of change,
When life is stark and bare and strange;
A solace when our eyes are wet
With tears of longing and regret.

True it is that we cannot claim
Unmeasured recompense or blame,
Because our way of life is small:
A little is the sum of all.

Anonymous

THE AGNOSTIC'S CREED

At last I have ceased repining, at last I accept my
fate;
I have ceased to beat at the Portal, I have ceased to
knock at the Gate;

I have ceased to work at the Puzzle, for the Secret
      has ended my search,
And I know that the Key is entrusted to never a
      creed nor church.

They have threatened with lakes of fire, they have
      threatened with fetters of hell;
They have offered me heights of heaven with their
      fields of asphodel;
But the Threat and the Bribe are useless if Reason
      be strong and stout,
And an honest man can never surrender an honest
      doubt.

The fables of hell and of heaven are but worn-out
      Christmas toys,
To coax or to bribe or to frighten the grown-up
      girls and boys;
I have ceased to be an infant, I have traveled be-
      yond their span —
It may do for women and children, but it never will
      do for a man.

They are all alike, these churches: Mohammedan,
      Christian, Parsee;
You are vile, you are curst, you are outcast, if you
      be not as they be;
But my Reason stands against them, and I go as it
      bids me go;
Its commands are as calls of a trumpet, and I follow
      for weal or woe.

But O! it is often cheerless, and O! it is often
    chill,
And I often sigh to heaven as my path grows steep
    and still.
I have left behind my comrades, with their prattle
    and childish noise;
My boyhood now is behind me, with all of its
    broken toys!

O! that God of gods is glorious, the emperor of
    every land;
He carries the moon and the planets in the palm of
    His mighty hand;
He is girt with the belt of Orion, he is Lord of the
    suns and stars,
A wielder of constellations, of Canopus, Arcturus
    and Mars!

I believe in Love and Duty, I believe in the True
    and Just;
I believe in the common kinship of everything born
    from dust.
I hope that the Right will triumph, that the scep-
    tered Wrong will fall.
That Death will at last be defeated, that the Grave
    will not end all.

I believe in the martyrs and heroes who have died
    for the sake of Right;
And I promise, like them, to follow in my Reason's
    faithful light;

If my Reason errs in judgment, I but honestly
     strive as I can;
If a God decrees my downfall, I shall stand it like a
     man.

Walter Malone

THE SUN-WORSHIPERS

The trail is high whereon we ride, with all the
     world below to see,
    The cleft of cañon, sweep of range and winter-
      white of lonely peak;
Lean foothold on the mountain-side, and on, be-
     yond, The Mystery,
    The unattained, the hidden land we may not find,
      but ever seek.

Content were vain. Our discontent, divine, forever
     urges on
    Through stress and danger, scorned or shared,
      though journey's end be never won:
Say you our days are vainly spent whose eyes have
     looked upon the dawn
    From high Chilao's morning crest, and bathed
      our faces in the Sun?

We worship not what men have made: no thing so
     small is our desire.
    The little words of men that die, the little
      thoughts of men that dream
Shall perish in their utterance: and build for these
     an altar fire?
    Our creed is written in the sky, our song in the
      eternal stream.

We journey on from star to star, nor shall we find a
dwelling-place,
Nor yet implore surcease from toil: to be and to
adore, is all:
Beholding dimly from afar the glory of the Hidden
Face,
Our worship ever our reward, the Quest our
golden coronal.

Henry Herbert Knibbs

A LAST APPEAL

O somewhere, somewhere, God unknown,
Exist and be!
I am dying; I am all alone;
I must have thee!

God! God! my sense, my soul, my all
Dies in the cry: —
Saw'st thou the faint star flame and fall?
Ah! it was I.

Frederic William Henry Myers

MY AIM

I live for those who love me, whose hearts are kind
and true,
For the heaven that smiles above me, and awaits
my spirit too;
For all human ties that bind me, for the task by
God assigned me;
For the bright hopes yet to find me and the good
that I can do.

I live to learn their story who suffered for my
 sake;
To emulate their glory and follow in their wake:
Bards, patriots, martyrs, sages, the heroic of all
 ages,
Whose deeds crowd history's pages, and Time's
 great volume make.

I live to hold communion with all that is divine,
To feel there is a union 'twixt nature's heart and
 mine;
To profit by affliction, reap truth from fields of fic-
 tion,
Grow wiser from conviction, and fulfil God's grand
 design.

I live to hail the season, by gifted ones foretold,
When man shall live by reason, and not alone by
 gold;
When man to man united, and every wrong thing
 righted,
The whole world shall be lighted, as Eden was of
 old.

I live for those who love me, for those who know me
 true;
For the heaven that smiles above me, and awaits
 my spirit too;
For the cause that lacks assistance, for the wrong
 that needs resistance,
For the future in the distance and the good that I
 can do.

G. Linnæus Banks

WE LODGE HIM IN THE MANGER

Yet if His Majesty, our sovereign lord,
Should of his own accord
Friendly himself invite,
And say "I'll be your guest to-morrow night,"
How should we stir ourselves, call and command
All hands to work! "Let no man idle stand.

"Set me fine Spanish tables in the hall;
See they be fitted all;
Let there be room to eat
And order taken that there want no meat.
See every sconce and candlestick made bright,
That without tapers they may give a light.

"Look to the presence: are the carpets spread,
The dazie o'er the head,
The cushions in the chairs,
And all the candles lighted on the stairs?
Perfume the chambers, and in any case
Let each man give attendance in his place!"

Thus, if a king were coming, would we do;
And 't were good reason too;
For 't is a duteous thing
To show all honour to an earthly king,
And after all our travail and our cost,
So he be pleased, to think no labour lost.

But at the coming of the King of Heaven
All's set at six and seven;
We wallow in our sin,
Christ cannot find a chamber in the inn.

We entertain Him always like a stranger,
And, as at first, still lodge Him in the manger.

Anonymous

IF THIS WERE FAITH!

God! If this were enough,
That I see things bare to the buff
And up to the buttocks in mire.
That I ask nor hope nor hire,
Not in the husk,
Nor dawn beyond the dusk,
Nor life beyond death:
God — if this were faith!

Having felt Thy wind in my face
Spit sorrow and disgrace,
Having seen Thy evil doom
In Golgotha and Khartoum,
And the brutes, the work of Thine hands,
Fill with injustice lands
And stain with blood the sea.
If still in my veins the glee
Of the black night and the sun
And the lost battle run;
If, an adept,
The iniquitous lists I still accept
With joy, and joy to endure and be withstood,
And still to battle and perish for a dream of good:
God — if that were enough!

If to feel in the ink of the slough
And the sink of the mire
Veins of glory and fire

Run through and transpierce and transpire,
And a secret purpose of glory fill each part,
And the answering glory of battle fill my heart;
To thrill with the joy of girded men,
To go on forever and fail, and go on again,
And be mauled to the earth and arise,
And contend for the shade of a word and a thing
      not seen with the eyes —
With the half of a broken hope for a pillow at night
That somehow the right is the right,
And the smooth shall bloom from the rough:
Lord — if that were enough!

Robert Louis Stevenson

DEFERRED

All things at last I win — but all too late,
  Like harvests gathered after he who sowed
  Has died of hunger; or a debt, long owed,
The creditor dead, paid heirs of his estate.

Upon my eyelids hangs a burning weight
  Of tears, now, looking on the long, long road
  And thinking of the slavery and the goad
In empty years when little things seemed great.

Is Hope's high goal a picture hung in air,
  The desert phantasm of the palm and Spring?
Yet even so, it still is real somewhere,
  And that foregleam is so divine a thing
  It works the forming of the spirit's wing —
Desire creative mastering all despair!

Stokely S. Fisher

"FEAR NOT THE MENACE"

Life as it is! Accept it; it is thine!
The God that gave it, gave it for thy good.
The God that made it had not been divine
Could he have set thee poison for thy food.

Abstain not; Life and Love, like night and day,
Offer themselves to us on their own terms,
— Not ours. Accept their bounty while ye may,
Before we be accepted by the worms.

We rail at Time and Chance, and break our hearts
To make the glory of to-day endure.
Is the sun dead because the day departs?
And are the suns of Life and Love less sure?

Fear not the menace of the bye-and-bye.
To-day is ours; to-morrow Fate must give.
Stretch out your hands and eat, although ye die!
Better to die than never once to live.

                              Richard Hovey

THROUGH NATURE UP TO GOD

Where once Zenobia's bastions rose,
    The wind that stirs the desert sand
Now softly sighs and sadly blows
    O'er Tadmor's desolated land; —
The dirge for life and glory fled,
The requiem for centuries dead.

The towers of Troy are sunk in tears,
    The golden domes of Tyre are gone,

And only wandering echo hears
    The vagrant name of Babylon;
And ravens flit and serpents hiss
O'er what was once Persepolis.
        •   •   •

Yet always the aspiring Soul, —
    The Angel in the mortal clod,
The Vision that defies control, —
    Will look through Nature up to God;
And strive, in word and form, to speak
The beauty it was born to seek.

And not in vain, from age to age,
    In forms of grandeur and of grace,
Is writ on more than History's page,
    The progress of the human race —
The rise of mind and feeling, shown
In golden poems made of stone.

William Winter

GOD IN MY GARDEN

A garden is a lovesome thing, God wot!
Rose plot,
    Fringed pool,
Fern'd grot —
    The veriest school
    Of peace; and yet the fool
Contends that God is not —
Not God! In gardens! When the eve is cool?
    Nay, but I have a sign;
    'T is very sure God walks in mine.

Thomas Edward Brown

A LITTLE WORK

A little work, a little play
To keep us going — and so, good-day!

A little warmth, a little light
Of love's bestowing — and so, good-night!

A little fun, to match the sorrow
Of each day's growing — and so, good-morrow!

A little trust that when we die
We reap our sowing! And so, good-bye!

George Du Maurier

THE DYING PANTHEIST TO THE PRIEST

Take your ivory Christ away:
   No dying god shall have my knee
While live gods breathe in this wild wind
   And shout from yonder dashing sea.

When March brings back the Adonis flower —
   No more the white processions meet
With incense to their risen lord
   About the pillared temple's feet.

From tusk of boar, from thrust of spear
   The dead rise not. At Eastertide
The same sun dances on their graves —
   Love's darling and the Crucified.

Yet still the year's returning tide
   Flows greenly round each ruined plinth,

Breaking on fallen shafts in foam
  Of crocus and of hyacinth:

Tossing a spray of swallows high,
  To flutter lightly on the breeze
And fleck with tiny spots of shade
  The sunshine on the broken frieze.

I know the gray-green asphodels
  Still sheet the dim Elysian mead,
And ever by dark Lethe's wells
  The poppy sheds her ghostly seed.

And once — O once! — when sunset lay
  Blood-red across the winter sea,
Where on the sands we drained our flasks
  And danced and cried our *Evoe!* —

Among the tossing cakes of ice
  And spouting of the frozen spray,
We saw their white limbs twist and whirl —
  The ancient sea-gods at their play.

The gold-brown liquor burned my heart,
  The icy tempest stung my brow:
The twanging of Apollo's lyre —
  I heard it as I hear it now.

O no, the old gods are not dead:
  I think that they will never die;
But I, who lie upon this bed
  In mortal anguish — what am I?

A wave that rises with a breath
  Above the infinite watery plain,
To foam and sparkle in the sun
  A moment ere it sink again.

The eternal undulation runs:
  A man, I die: perchance to be,
Next life, a white-throat on the wind,
  A daffodil on Tempe's lea.

They lied who said that Pan was dead:
  Life was, life is, and life shall be.
So take away your crucifix —
  The everliving gods for me!
                                    Henry A. Beers

THE SEEKER

The creeds he wrought of dream and thought
  Fall from him at the touch of life,
  His old gods fail him in the strife —
Withdrawn, the heavens he sought!

Vanished the miracles that led,
  The cloud at noon, the flame at night;
The vision that he wing'd and sped
  Falls backward, baffled, from the height;

Yet in the wreck of these he stands
  Upheld by something grim and strong;
  Some stubborn instinct lifts a song
And nerves him, heart and hands;

He does not dare to call it hope; —
  It is not aught that seeks reward —

Nor faith, that up some sunward slope
   Runs aureoled to meet its lord;

It touches something elder far
   Than faith or creed or thought in man,
   It was ere yet these lived and ran
Like light from star to star;

It touches that stark, primal need
   That from unpeopled voids and vast,
Fashioned the first crude, childish creed, —
   And still shall fashion, till the last!

For one word is the tale of men:
   They fling their ikons to the sod,
   And having trampled down a god
They seek a god again!

Stripped of his creeds inherited,
   Bereft of all his sires held true,
Amid the wreck of visions dead
   He thrills at touch of visions new. . . .

He wings another Dream for flight. . . .
   He seeks beyond the outmost dawn
   A god he set there . . . and, anon,
Drags that god from the height!

But aye from ruined faiths and old
   That droop and die, fall bruisèd seeds;
And when new flowers and faiths unfold,
   They're lovelier flowers, they're kindlier
    creeds.

                  Don Marquis

"ALIENI TEMPORIS FLORES"

*("And wise men hold in due respect
the blossoms of other days.")*

Let the dead past bury its dead?
No one denies the need of this,
The utter childlike human need;
Nor that dead dreams, dead tears, dead loves,
Should lie perdu
Within the vault of time;
Nor that the snows of other years
Must melt away
Before the hot procession of our headlong days.

But let it be no more than this;
Let us not seize upon the hours
When blood ran tumbling to the lips,
And make of memory a thing of scorn;
Let us not taint the honest wine of old desire
With cheap regret:
The cheapest pain within all mortal range;
Let us not say that where we gave and took,
Full-hearted and full-hoped and daring all,
The world was aught the poorer for our dreams.

Let the dead past bury its dead?
Yes — but in full honor, too!
Not only for the flame that was its breath,
But for the spark
That somewhere smolders in the grave.

G. B. C.

MAKE NO DESPERATE SEARCH
FOR GOD

Come out to our house any week-end in June,
When dandelions riot in the grass:
And drink the yellow floods of afternoon,
Poured from a sky of blue and quivering glass.
Go through the arbor where the ramblers mass
In crimson flame against white lattices:
Open the easy swinging gate, and pass
Beneath the birch, between the maple trees
With tops a-tremble in the southwest breeze:
Follow along the curving gravel walk
Up to the terrace top, where, as you please,
Tobacco, high adventure, casual talk,
And journey's end await, if you are one
Who would live much and quietly in the sun.

. . .

On Sunday morning you may go to church
In any way you please, or not at all.
There is a stately one beneath our birch,
A lowlier one out by the garden wall:
Methodist, Catholic, Episcopal,
Are all within an easy morning's stroll;
But if these venerable creeds appal,
A garden spade may benefit your soul;
Or some eternal verity unroll
As you spread paint upon the kitchen screens,
Or fix fresh-cut nasturtiums in a bowl,
Or hold communion with the lima beans.
Or you may put your clean white flannels on
And meet it as you ramble through the lawn.

But do not make a desperate search for God
Lest you offend his quiet dignity.
The week-end is no time to pant or plod
The rock-strewn roads of any Calvary.
It is a time to live in the sun, and see
Your favorite god by glimpses, everywhere.
I find him lurking quite persistently
In our young daughter's laugh, and in her hair;
And if the baby smiles, he lingers there:
But when the baby cries, he understands
And straightway slips without offense or care
Into my wife's brown eyes and her white hands;
And many a moonlit night in fall he comes
To dance among the red chrysanthemums.

John French Wilson

JESUS THE CARPENTER

"Is n't this Joseph's son?" — ay, it is He;
Joseph the carpenter — same trade as me —
I thought as I'd find it — I knew it was here —
    But my sight's getting queer.

I don't know right where as his shed must ha'
        stood —
But often, as I've been a-planing my wood,
I've took off my hat, just with thinking of He
    At the same work as me.

He warn't that set up that He could n't stoop
        down
And work in the country for folks in the town;
And I'll warrant He felt a bit pride, like I've done
    At a good job begun.

The parson he knows that I'll not make too free,
But on Sunday I feels as pleased as can be,
When I wears my clean smock, and sits in a pew,
    And has thoughts a few.

I think of as how not the parson hissen,
As is teacher and father and shepherd o' men,
Not he knows as much of the Lord in that shed,
    Where He earned his own bread.

And when I goes home to my missus, says she,
" Are ye wanting your key?"
For she knows my queer ways, and my love for the
    shed,
    (We've been forty years wed.)

So I comes right away by mysen, with the book,
And I turns the old pages and has a good look
For the text as I've found, as tells me as He
    Were the same trade as me.

Why don't I mark it? Ah, many says so,
But I think I'd as lief, with your leave, let it go:
It do seem that nice when I fall on it sudden —
    Unexpected, you know!
                   Catherine C. Liddell

ATOMS AND AGES

    Just as I wonder at the twofold screen
    Of twisted innocence that you would plait
    For eyes that uncourageously await
    The coming of a kingdom that has been,

So do I wonder what God's love can mean
To you that all so strangely estimate
The purpose and the consequent estate
Of one short shuddering step to the Unseen.

No, I have not your backward faith to shrink
Lone-faring from the doorway of God's home
To find Him in the names of buried men;
Nor your ingenious recreance to think
We cherish, in the life that is to come,
The scattered features of dead friends again.

Never until our souls are strong enough
To plunge into the crater of the Scheme —
Triumphant in the flash there to redeem
Love's handsel — and forevermore to slough,
Like cerements at a played-out masque, the
     rough
And reptile skins of us whereon we set
The stigma of scared years — are we to get
Where atoms and the ages are one stuff.

Nor ever shall we know the cursèd waste
Of life in the beneficence divine
Of starlight and of sunlight and soul-shine
That we have squandered in sin's frail distress,
Till we have drunk, and trembled at the taste,
The mead of Thought's prophetic endlessness.
                    Edwin Arlington Robinson

THE PAGAN

But I shall feel the wind again,
 Shall drink the scent of flower and pine:
And I shall bask in April suns
 Where budding willow boughs are mine,
The stars will beat across the night,
 The waves will shout their tumult then;
And I shall answer in my joy,
 My joy at praising life again.

For I have lived with waving grass
 And roots and golden sap astir;
The earth has held me to her breast,
 And I shall laugh again with her.
I have loved clouds that drift and pass,
 My heart has flamed to eager bloom
In gold and crimson poppy leaves
 And rose perfume.

And I shall dance beneath the light
 Of silver crescent moons in spring,
And I shall sleep upon the leaves
 Of autumn's yellow mouldering.
For somewhere, there will open wide
 A little magic, outer door,
And I shall pass beyond to find
 The loveliness I knew before.

Rose Henderson

"HE WHOM A DREAM HATH POSSESSED"

He whom a dream hath possessed knoweth no
more of doubting,
For mist and the blowing of winds and the mouth-
ing of words he scorns;
Not the sinuous speech of schools he hears, but a
knightly shouting,
And never comes darkness down, yet he greeteth
a million morns.

He whom a dream hath possessed knoweth no
more of roaming;
All roads and the flowing of waves and the speed-
iest flight he knows;
But wherever his feet are set, his soul is forever
homing,
And going, he comes; and coming, he heareth a
call and goes.

He whom a dream hath possessed knoweth no
more of sorrow,
At death and the dropping of leaves and the fading of suns he smiles,
For a dream remembers no past and scorns the desire of a morrow,
And a dream in a sea of doom sets surely the
ultimate isles.

He whom a dream hath possessed treads the im-
palpable marches,
From the dust of the day's long road he leaps to a
laughing star,

And the ruin of worlds that fall he views from eternal arches,
And rides God's battle-field in a flashing and
golden car.

Shaemas O'Sheel

APRIL THEOLOGY

Oh to be breathing and hearing and feeling and
seeing!
Oh the ineffably glorious privilege of being!
All of the World's lovely girlhood, unfleshed and
made spirit,
Broods out in the sunlight this morning — I see it,
I hear it!

So read me no text, O my Brothers, and preach me
no creeds;
I am busy beholding the glory of God in His deeds!
See! Everywhere buds coming out, blossoms flaming, bees humming!
Glad athletic growers up-reaching, things striving,
becoming!

Oh, I know in my heart, in the sun-quickened,
blossoming soul of me,
This something called self is a part, but the world is
the whole of me!
I am one with these growers, these singers, these
earnest becomers —
Co-heirs of the summer to be and past æons of
summers!

I kneel not nor grovel; no prayer with my lips shall
    I fashion.
Close-knit in the fabric of things, fused with one
    common passion —
To go on and become something greater — we
    growers are one;
None more in the world than a bird and none less
    than the sun;
But all woven into the glad indivisible Scheme,
God fashioning out in the Finite a part of his
    dream!

Out here where the world-love is flowing, unfet-
    tered, unpriced,
I feel all the depth of the man-soul and girl-heart
    of Christ!
'Mid this riot of pink and white flame in this mira-
    cle weather,
Soul to soul, merged in one, God and I dream the
    vast dream together.
We are one in the doing of things that are done and
    to be:
I am part of my God as a raindrop is part of the sea!

What! House me my God? Take me in where no
    blossoms are blowing?
Roof me in from the blue, wall me in from the
    green and the wonder of growing?
Parcel out what already is mine, like a vendor of
    staples?
*See! Yonder my God burns revealed in the sap-
    drunken maples!*

                                    John G. Neihardt

THE CERTAIN VICTORY

Why should I sit in doubt or fear? If I
  Awake some morning from that dreaded sleep
To find myself new-born and lifted high,
  Then I will turn, and, looking o'er the deep
That lies beneath me, shout for glee and throw
  A last good-by at Pain and Fear, below.

But what if, at the last, no light shall break —
  If this is all — if when I fall asleep
No angel's voice shall sweetly cry "Awake,"
  And there shall be but Nothing, dark and
    deep —
Ah, well, I shall not care if it be so,
  I'll triumph still, for I shall never know.

S. E. Kiser

"THE VISION SPLENDID"

Our birth is but a sleep and a forgetting:
The Soul that rises with us, our life's Star,
  Hath had elsewhere its setting,
    And cometh from afar:
  Not in entire forgetfulness,
  And not in utter nakedness,
But trailing clouds of glory do we come
  From God, who is our home:
Heaven lies about us in our infancy!
Shades of the prison-house begin to close
  Upon the growing Boy,
But He beholds the light, and whence it flows,
  He sees it in his joy;

The Youth, who daily farther from the east
   Must travel, still is Nature's Priest,
   And by the Vision Splendid
   Is on his way attended;
At length the Man perceives it die away,
And fade into the light of common day.

Wordsworth

"SAY NOT THE STRUGGLE NAUGHT AVAILETH"

Say not the struggle naught availeth,
   The labour and the wounds are vain,
The enemy faints not, nor faileth,
   And as things have been they remain.

If hopes were dupes, fears may be liars;
   It may be, in yon smoke conceal'd,
Your comrades chase e'en now the flyers,
   And, but for you, possess the field.

For while the tired waves, vainly breaking,
   Seem here no painful inch to gain,
Far back, through creeks and inlets making,
   Comes silent, flooding in, the main.

And not by eastern windows only,
   When daylight comes, comes in the light;
In front the sun climbs slow, how slowly!
   But westward, look, the land is bright!

Arthur Hugh Clough

MIMNERMUS IN CHURCH

You promise heavens free from strife,
    Pure truth, and perfect change of will;
But sweet, sweet is this human life,
    So sweet, I fain would breathe it still:
Your chilly stars I can forego,
This warm, kind world is all I know.

You say there is no substance here,
    One great reality above:
Back from that void I shrink in fear,
    And child-like hide myself in love:
Show me what angels feel. Till then,
I cling, a mere weak man, to men.

You bid me lift my mean desires
    From faltering lips and fitful veins
To sexless souls, ideal choirs,
    Unwearied voices, wordless strains:
My mind with fonder welcome owns
One dear, dead friend's remembered tones.

Forsooth the present we must give
    To that which cannot pass away;
All beauteous things for which we live
    By laws of time and space decay.
But oh, the very reason why
I clasp them, is because they die.

                    William Johnson Cory

THE SCIENTIST SPEAKS

First, I abjure all dim unreasoning patter
  Wherewith the ignorant befool their kind;
Because I read among the Laws of Matter
  The limitations of the human mind.

Then I will not believe, till I have cloven
  Into the very heart of Law and Act;
That no one need accept what I have proven
  Till he has put it to the proof of Fact.

Nor will I let the teachings of another
  Absolve me from my task of finding out,
Just as I will not force upon my brother
  The answer I have made to mine own doubt.

I will be true to this, though all may doubt me,
  I will write on, and over every sneer.
So will I build my Heaven here about me
  And live my life within it, now and here.
                    Charles Henry Mackintosh

"CORONEMUS NOS ROSIS ANTEQUAM MARCESCANT"

Let us drink and be merry, dance, joke, and re-
      joice,
With claret and sherry, theorbo and voice!
The changeable world to our joy is unjust,
    All treasure's uncertain,
    Then down with your dust!
In frolics dispose your pounds, shillings, and pence,
For we shall be nothing a hundred years hence.

We'll sport and be free with Moll, Betty, and Dolly,
Have oysters and lobsters to cure melancholy:
Fish-dinners will make a man spring like a flea,
    Dame Venus, love's lady,
    Was born of the sea:
With her and with Bacchus we'll tickle the sense,
For we shall be past it a hundred years hence.

Your most beautiful bride who with garlands is
    crowned
And kills with each glance as she treads on the
    ground,
Whose lightness and brightness doth shine in such
    splendor
    That none but the stars
    Are thought fit to attend her,
Though now she be pleasant and sweet to the
    sense,
Will be damnable mouldy a hundred years hence.

Then why should we turmoil in cares and in fears,
Turn all our tranquill'ty to sighs and to tears?
Let's eat, drink and play till the worms do corrupt
    us,
    'T is certain, *"Post mortem*
    Nulla voluptas."
For health, wealth, and beauty, wit, learning and
    sense,
Must all come to nothing a hundred years hence.
                   Thomas Jordan

WINE OF OMAR KHAYYÁM

He rode the flame-winged dragon-steed of Thought
　　Through Space and Darkness, seeking Heav'n
　　　　and Hell;
　　And searched the furthest stars where souls
　　　　might dwell
To find God's justice; and in vain he sought.

Then, looking on the dusk-eyed girl who brought
　　His dream-filled wine beside his garden well,
　　He said: "Her kiss; the wine-jug's drowsy spell;
Bulbul; the roses; death; — all else is naught:

"So drink till that." — What! drink, because the
　　abyss
　　Of Nothing waits? Because there is for man
But one swift hour of consciousness and light?

No — just because we have no life but this,
　　Turn it to use; be noble while you can;
Search, help, create; then pass into the night.
　　　　　　　　　　　　　Eugene Lee-Hamilton

THE PROBLEM

I like a church; I like a cowl;
I love a prophet of the soul;
And on my heart monastic aisles
Fall like sweet strains, or pensive smiles:
Yet not for all his faith can see
Would I that cowlèd churchman be.
Why should the vest on him allure,
Which I could not on me endure?

Not from a vain or shallow thought
His awful Jove young Phidias brought;
Never from lips of cunning fell
The thrilling Delphic oracle;
Out from the heart of Nature rolled
The burdens of the Bible old;
The litanies of nations came,
Like the volcano's tongue of flame,
Up from the burning core below, —
The canticles of love and woe:
The hand that rounded Peter's dome,
And groined the aisles of Christian Rome,
Wrought in a sad sincerity;
Himself from God he could not free;
He builded better than he knew; —
The conscious stone to beauty grew.

Know'st thou what wove yon woodbird's nest
Of leaves, and feathers from her breast?
Or how the fish outbuilt her shell,
Painting with morn each annual cell?
Or how the sacred pine-tree adds
To her old leaves new myriads?
Such and so grew these holy piles,
Whilst love and terror laid the tiles.
Earth proudly wears the Parthenon,
As the best gem upon her zone,
And Morning opes with haste her lids,
To gaze upon the Pyramids;
O'er England's abbeys bends the sky,
As on its friends, with kindred eye;
For, out of Thought's interior sphere,
These wonders rose to upper air;

And Nature gladly gave them place,
Adopted them into her race,
And granted them an equal date
With Andes and with Ararat.

These temples grew as grows the grass;
Art might obey, but not surpass.
The passive Master lent his hand
To the vast soul that o'er him planned;
And the same power that reared the shrine
Bestrode the tribes that knelt within.
Ever the fiery Pentecost
Girds with one flame the countless host,
Trances the heart through chanting choirs,
And through the priest the mind inspires.
The word unto the prophet spoken
Was writ on tables yet unbroken;
The word by seers or sibyls told,
In groves of oak, or fanes of gold,
Still floats upon the morning wind,
Still whispers to the willing mind.
One accent of the Holy Ghost
The heedless world hath never lost.
I know what say the fathers wise, —
The Book itself before me lies, —
Old *Chrysostom,* best Augustine,
And he who blent both in his line,
The younger *Golden Lips* or mines,
Taylor, the Shakespeare of divines.
His words are music in my ear,
I see his cowlèd portrait dear;
And yet, for all his faith could see,
I would not the good bishop be.

                              Ralph Waldo Emerson

THE PHANTOM CARAVAN

And if the wine you drink, the lip you press,
End in what all begins and ends in — Yes;
   Think then you are To-day what Yesterday
You were — To-morrow you shall not be less.

So when the Angel of the darker drink
At last shall find you by the river-brink,
   And, offering his cup, invite your Soul
Forth to your lips to quaff — you shall not shrink.

Why, if the Soul can fling the dust aside,
And naked on the air of Heaven ride,
   Wer't not a shame — wer't not a shame for
       him
In this clay carcase crippled to abide?

'T is but a tent where takes his one-day's rest
A Sultan to the realm of Death addrest;
   The Sultan rises, and the dark Ferrash
Strikes, and prepares it for another guest.

And fear not lest existence closing your
Account, and mine, should know the like no more;
   The Eternal Saki from that bowl has pour'd
Millions of bubbles like us, and will pour.

When you and I behind the veil are past,
Oh but the long long while the world shall last
   Which of our coming and departure heeds
As the Sev'n Seas should heed a pebble-cast.

A moment's halt — a momentary taste
Of Being from the well amid the waste —
   And lo! — the phantom caravan has reach'd
The Nothing it set out from — Oh, make haste!
             Omar Khayyâm
      Translated by Edward Fitzgerald

THE MOVING FINGER WRITES

I sent my soul through the invisible,
Some letter of that after-life to spell:
   And by and by my Soul return'd to me,
And answer'd: "I myself am Heav'n and Hell."

Heav'n but the vision of fulfill'd desire,
And Hell the shadow of a soul on fire,
   Cast on the darkness into which ourselves,
So late emerged from, shall so soon expire.

We are no other than a moving row
Of magic shadow-shapes that come and go
   Round with this sun-illumin'd lantern held
In midnight by the Master of the Show;

Impotent pieces of the game He plays
Upon this checker-board of nights and days;
   Hither and thither moves, and checks, and
     slays,
And one by one back in the closet lays.

The ball no question makes of ayes and noes
But right and left as strikes the Player goes;
   And He that toss'd you down into the field,
He knows about it all — He knows — He knows!

The Moving Finger writes; and, having writ,
Moves on: nor all your piety nor wit
    Shall lure it back to cancel half a line,
Nor all your tears wash out a word of it.

And that inverted bowl they call the Sky,
Whereunder crawling coop'd we live and die,
    Lift not your hands to It for help — for It
As impotently rolls as you or I.

Omar Khayyam
Translated by Edward Fitzgerald

NIRVANA

Sleep will He give His beloved?
  Not dreams, but the precious guerdon of deepest
    rest?
Aye, surely! Look on the grave-closed eyes,
  And cold hands folded on tranquil breast.
Will *not* the All-Great be just and forgive?
  For He knows (though we make no prayer nor
    cry)
How our lone souls ached when our pale star waned,
  How we watch the promiseless sky.
Life hereafter? Ah, no: we have lived enough.
  Life eternal? Pray God it may *not* be so.
Have we not suffered and striven, loved and en-
    dured,
  Run through the whole wide gamut of passion
    and woe?

Strangest illusion! Sprung from a fevered habit of
  hope —
  Wild enthusiast's dream of blatant perfection at
    best

Give us darkness for anguished eyes, stillness for
    weary feet,
  Silence and sleep; but no heaven of glittering,
    loud unrest.
No more the life-long labour of smoothing the
    stone-strewn way;
  No more the shuddering outlook athwart the
    sterile plain,
Where every step we take, every word we say,
  Each warm, living hand that we cling to, is but a
    fence against pain.

And nothing may perish, but lives again? Where?
    Out of thought, out of sight?
And where is your cresset's flame that the rough
    wind slew last night?
        Rosamund Marriott Watson

STARS IN THE MIST

I have followed the sins of reckless youth
  With the Devil to time the dance,
And farther and farther I drift from Truth
  As the hopeless years advance;
Round me and over the mists are spread,
  With the pathway hard to find,
And the roar of the flames of Hell ahead
  And the bridges burnt behind.

But I ask no help of the gods on high,
  On the Devil I will not lean,
And I will not drop to my knees, not I,
  For the whole world in between;

For, a-shine on the gates of the Future barred,
  Two stars in the darkness move
To guide me: the star of a man's regard
  And the star of a woman's love.

I shall know no doubt, I shall hold no fear,
  I shall suffer and make no sign,
As long as those stars in the night burn clear
  And the way of those stars be mine;
And I shall go down to the Deep Abyss
  With a scorn of the fears of old
If Fortune will leave me that true girl's kiss
  And that true man's hand to hold.

Will H. Ogilvie

ONE PATH

Outside the Earthly Paradise,
  Beneath its great gold walls,
I walk a little, grass-blurred path
  Where sunlight seldom falls.

I try no more the guarded gates
  That will not let me in;
I cease to wonder what the cause,
  What accident, or sin.

I walk the lonely path that's mine,
  My heart and I employ
Our solitude in songs that hymn
  The near-by Kingdom's joy.

And once while singing thus, we heard
  Far-off and friendly cries

And saw, high up, our happy kin,
  Love in their lovely eyes.

Then on alone! . . . Where leads my path
  Or ends I can not tell;
Outside the Earthly Paradise
  I know, — but that is well.

                    William Alexander Percy

KRITERION

I see the spire,
    I see the throng,
I hear the choir,
    I hear the song;
I listen to the anthem, while
It pours its volume down the aisle;
  I listen to the splendid rhyme
  That, with a melody sublime,
  Tells of some far-off, fadeless clime —
    Of man and his finality,
    Of hope, and immortality.

    Oh, theme of themes!
      Are men mistaught?
    Are hopes like dreams,
      To come to naught?
Is all the beautiful and good
Delusive and misunderstood?
  And has the soul no forward reach?
  And do indeed the facts impeach
  The theories the teachers teach?
    And is this immortality
    Delusion or reality?

What hope reveals
　　Mind tries to clasp,
But soon it reels
　　With broken grasp.
No chain yet forged on anvil's brink
Was stronger than its weakest link;
　　And are there not along this chain
　　Imperfect links that snap in twain
　　When caught in logic's tensile strain?
　　　And is not immortality
　　　The child of ideality?

And yet — at times —
　　We get advice
That seems like chimes
　　From paradise;
The soul doth sometimes seem to be
In sunshine which it cannot see;
　　At times the spirit seems to roam
　　Beyond the land, above the foam,
　　Back to some half-forgotten home.
　　　Perhaps — this immortality
　　　May be indeed reality.

Eugene F. Ware

NOTHINGNESS

Behind the hosts of suns and stars, behind
The rushing of the chariots of the wind,
Behind all noises and all shapes of things,
And men and deeds — behind the blaze of kings,
Princes and paladins and potentates —
An immense, solitary Spectre waits.

It has no shape: it has no sound: it has
No place: it has no time: it is, and was,
And will be: it is never more nor less,
Nor glad, nor sad. Its name is Nothingness.
Power walketh high: and Misery doth crawl:
And the clepsydra drips: and the sands fall
Down in the hour-glass: and the shadows sweep
Around the dial: and men wake, and sleep,
Live, strive, regret, forget, and love, and hate,
And know it not. This spectre saith: "I wait."
And at last it beckons, and they pass.
And still the red sands fall within the glass:
And still the shades around the dial sweep:
And still the water-clock doth drip and weep:
And this is all.

Owen Meredith

THE AWAKENING

I

Outward from the planets are blown the fumes of
    thought,
And the breath of prayer drifts out and makes a
    mist between the stars;

The void shall be void no longer,
And the caverns of infinity shall be fulfilled of
    spirit;

For in the wilderness between the worlds a sen-
    tience struggles to awaken,
Passions and ghosts and visions gather into a
    Form.

The God that we have worshipped for a million
     years begins to be,
And he whom we have prayed to creates himself
     out of the stuff of our prayers.

His wings are still heavy with chaos,
And his pinions are holden down as with a weight of
     slumber;

His face is ambiguous,
His countenance is uncertain behind the veils of
     space;

He has not speech,
He has but only thunder for his voice;

But the mornings gather to shape his eye,
And the fire of many dawns has thrilled his twilight
     with a prescience of vision.

II

From myriad altars a reek of incense,
And outward from the constellations there leaps
     the flame of burning prophets;

There goes forth the breath of lovely purpose,
As a south wind bearing seeds over a meadow it
     goes forth across the firmament;

There arises a dew from the bruised foreheads of
     martyrs,
And the broken hearts of the just, of them that have
     loved justice, are dissolved into a bloody
     dew;

Out from the populated spheres a mist,
And from the peopled worlds a breeding fog:

And in the mist a God gathers unto Himself Form,
    and apparels himself in Being;
For they that have desired a God create him from
    the stuff of that desire.

III

In the nebular chasms there is a shaping soul,
And a light begins to glow in the dark abyss;

That which is to be draws to itself what has been
    and what is,
He drinks up the hopes of them that were as a sun
    sucks up water;

He builds himself out of the desperate faith of
    them that have sought him,
And his face shall be wrought of the wish to see his
    face.

Man has lifted his voice unto the hollow sky and
    there was no answer but the echo of his voice,
But out of many echoes there shall grow a word.

There is a cry from the peaks of Caucasus,
From the throat of Prometheus a hoarse shout of
    agony and courage and defiance;

Answer, O you stars! and make reply, you rushing
    worlds!
Have you not always chained your Titans where
    the vultures scream about the bloodied
    rocks

Have you not thrust your beaks into the livers of
      them that loved you?

There is a cry goes forth from all the stars,
The voice of rebels and great lovers;

Out of agonies and love shall God be made,
He is wrought of cries that meet between the
      worlds,
Of seeking cries that have come forth from the
      cruel spheres to find a God and be stilled.

Answer, you populations,
And make reply, you planets that are red in space:
Do not ten thousand broken Christs this hour cry
      their despair?

Are not Golgothas shaken this hour and the suns
      shamed?
Goes there not forth a manifold wailing of them
      that cry;
"My God, my God, why hast thou forsaken me?"

These cries have wandered out along the waste
      places,
And these despairs have met in the wilderness of
      chaos,
And they have wrought a God;

For he builds himself of the passion of martyrs,
And he is woven of the ecstasy of great lovers,
And he is wrought of the anguish of them that have
      greatly needed him.

Don Marquis

THE KASIDAH

(The Lay of the Higher Law)

Do what thy manhood bids thee do, from none but
self expect applause;
He noblest lives and noblest dies who makes and
keeps his self-made laws.

All other Life is living Death, a world where none
but Phantoms dwell,
A breath, a wind, a sound, a voice, a tinkling of the
camel's-bell.

· · ·

And, glancing down the range of years, fear not thy
future self to see;
Resign'd to life, to death resign'd, as though the
choice were naught to thee.

Pluck the old woman from thy breast; Be stout in
woe, be stark in weal;
Do good for Good is good to do: Spurn bribe of
Heav'n and threat of Hell.

To seek the True, to glad the heart, such is of life
the HIGHER LAW,
Whose diff'rence is the Man's degree, the Man of
gold, the Man of straw.

See not that something in Mankind that rouses
hate or scorn or strife,
Better the worm of Izrail than Death that walks in
form of Life.

Survey thy kind as One whose wants in the great
    Human Whole unite;
The Homo rising high from earth to seek the
    Heav'ns of Life-in-Light;

And hold Humanity one man, whose universal
    agony
Still strains and strives to gain the goal, where
    agonies shall cease to be.

Believe in all things; none believe; judge not nor
    warp by "Facts" the thought;
See clear, hear clear, tho' life may seem Maya and
    Mirage, Dream and Naught.

Abjure the Why and seek the How: the God and
    gods enthroned on high
Are silent all, are silent still; nor hear thy voice, nor
    deign reply.

· · ·

Perchance the law some Giver hath: Let be! let be!
    what canst thou know?
A myriad races came and went; this Sphinx hath
    seen them come and go.

Haply the Law that rules the world allows to man
    the widest range;
And haply Fate's a Theist-word, subject to human
    chance and change.

This "I" may find a future life, a nobler copy of our
    own,
Where every riddle shall be ree'd, where every
    knowledge shall be known;

Where 'twill be man's to see the whole of what on
   Earth he sees in part;
Where change shall ne'er surcharge the thought;
   nor hope defer'd shall hurt the heart.

But! — faded flower and fallen leaf no more shall
   deck the parent tree;
And man once dropt by Tree of Life what hope of
   mother life has he?

The shatter'd bowl shall know repair; the riven lute
   shall sound once more;
But who shall mend the clay of man, the stolen
   breath to man restore?

The shiver'd clock again shall strike; the broken
   reed shall pipe again:
But we, we die, and Death is one, the doom of
   brutes, the doom of men.

Then, if Nirwana round our life with nothingness,
   't is haply best;
Thy toils and troubles, want and woe at length have
   won their guerdon — Rest.

. . .

Wend now thy way with brow serene, fear not thy
   humble tale to tell: —
The whispers of the Desert-wind; the Tinkling of
   the camel's-bell.

        Sir Richard Burton

DISSOLUTION

If he may come for me;
If, when the ebbing tide runs out to sea,
He'll come from out the gloom, once more, and
      stand
There, close beside me, holding out his hand;
If I may see, ere blackness closes in,
The reassurance of his boyish grin —
I shall have grace to smile on those who weep,
And close my eyes in sleep.

If he will speak my name,
It will not be as though Death's Angel came,
Stern-eyed and winged with flame, to take me
      home —
For there are purple hills we loved to roam;
We knew calm streams with shoals where fishes
      spawn,
And sunsets' fires and bugles of the dawn,
And tranquil pools, inviting us to swim —
So, I would welcome him.

I would not that my eyes
Should see him in the garb of Paradise,
Serene and radiant, with the earthly clay
By fires of tribulation burned away,
A splendid spirit, bright and purified;
Nor with the smile that came the day he died —
That strange, high smile of cold austerity;
I pray this may not be.

I hope he may not speak
Some august, sounding summons to the weak

And frightened spirit. Let his battered creel
Be slung and in his hand his rod and reel.
So let me see him stand there, kind and fat,
With grizzled hair and trout-flies in his hat,
And, bending, grin and slap my back and say:
"Come, son; they'll rise to-day!"

Frederic F. Van de Water

"UNTO THE LEAST OF THESE"

The Lord was teaching folk by the sea shore;
His voice had quelled the storm, it raged no
     more;
His word was like a balm, and did impart
Joy to the righteous, hope to the broken heart.
"Whoso shall love me perfectly," said He,
"Shall look upon my Father and on Me."
And people listened humbly to His Word.

Now on the outer side of them that heard,
A certain woman, leading by the hand
Her child, had halted, passing on that way,
And hearkening for a while the twain did stand.
She had grown old with gleaning, and that day
The load she carried was of straw, not wheat,
And all her mother's heart heaved full of sighs;
But lo, the boy was rosy-hued and sweet;
A fair, small child he was, with smiling eyes
That shamed the miserable rags he wore.
The child said: "Mother, who speaks there on
     the shore?"
"Child, 't is a prophet: holy laws they be
He gives to men."

"I wish that I could see
The prophet, mother." And the child strove
    hard,
Stood on tiptoe, and pressed to find a breach
In the thick crowd; but many tall folk barred
And hemmed him in, so that he could not
    reach
To look upon the Master whose kind speech
Wrought in his ear. Then, eager still, he cried:
"I should behold him, mother dear, if thou
Wouldst lift me in thine arms."

                  But she replied,
"Child, I am tired; I cannot lift thee now."
Then a great sadness came upon the child
And tears stood in the eyes that lately smiled.

But Jesus, walking through the crowd, drew
    near
E'en to the child and said, "Lo, — I am here."
               Arthur O'Shaughnessy

"HE GIVETH HIS BELOVED SLEEP"

The long day passes with its load of sorrow:
    In slumber deep
I lay me down to rest until to-morrow —
    Thank God for sleep.

Thank God for all respite from weary toiling,
    From cares that creep
Across our lives like evil shadows, spoiling
    God's kindly sleep.

We plough and sow, and, as the hours grow
    later,
      We strive to reap,
And build our barns, and hope to build them
    greater
      Before we sleep.

We toil and strain and strive with one another
      In hopes to heap
Some greater share of profit than our brother
      Before we sleep.

What will it profit that with tears or laughter
      Our watch we keep?
Beyond it all there lies the Great Hereafter —
      Thank God for sleep!

For, at the last, beseeching Christ to save us,
      We turn with deep,
Heart-felt thanksgiving unto God who gave us
      The Gift of Sleep.

                Major A. B. Paterson

THE HILLS OF REST

Beyond the last horizon's rim,
    Beyond adventure's farthest quest,
Somewhere they rise, serene and dim,
    The happy, happy Hills of Rest.

Upon their sunlit slopes uplift
    The castles we have built in Spain —
While fair amid the summer drift
    Our faded gardens flower again.

Sweet hours we did not live go by
    To soothing note, on scented wing;
In golden-lettered volumes lie
    The songs we tried in vain to sing.

They all are there: the days of dream
    That build the inner lives of men;
The silent, sacred years we deem
    The might be, and the might have been.

Some evening when the sky is gold
    I'll follow day into the west;
Nor pause, nor heed, till I behold
    The happy, happy Hills of Rest.
                 Albert Bigelow Paine

"DAREST THOU NOW, O SOUL"

Darest thou now, O soul,
Walk out with me toward the unknown region,
Where neither ground is for the feet nor any path to
    follow?

No map there, nor guide,
Nor voice sounding, nor touch of human hand,
Nor face with blooming flesh, nor lips, nor eyes, are
    in that land.

I know it not, O soul!
Nor dost thou, all is a blank before us, —
All waits undreamed of in that region, that inacces-
    sible land.

Till when the tie is loosened,
All but the ties eternal, Time and Space,
Nor darkness, gravitation, sense, nor any bounds
      bounding us —

Then we burst forth, we float,
In Time and Space, O soul! prepared for them,
Equal, equipped at last, — O joy! O fruit of all! —
      them to fulfill, O soul!

                   Walt Whitman

"WHEN THE TIME FOR PARTING COMES"

When the time for parting comes, and the day is on
      the wane,
And the silent evening darkens over hill and over
      plain,
And earth holds no more sorrow, no more grief, and
      no more pain,
    Shall we weary for the battle and the strife?

When at last the trail is ending, and the stars are
      growing near,
And we breathe the breath of conquest, and the
      voices that we hear
Are the great companions' voices that have hal-
      lowed year on year,
    Shall we know an instant's grieving as we pass?

Shall we pause a fleeting moment ere we grasp the
      eager hands,
Take one last long look of wonder at the dimming of
      the lands,

Love the earth one glowing moment ere we pass
    from its demands,
  Cull all beauty in its essence as we gaze?

Or with not one backward longing shall we leap the
    last abyss,
Scale the highest crags glad-hearted, fearful only
    lest the bliss
Of an earth-remembering instant should delay the
    great sun's kiss —
  Consuming us within the splendor of the flame?
              Dorothea Lawrance Mann

EPITAPH

That my great friend should lie
Blind to the morning sky,
The bold, persistent glory of the sun;
That men should say,
"Brave was his day,
Yet now his day is done,"

Is the true grief I bear . . .
Not for my selfish share
In his keen mind, high heart, courageous
    life;
Sorrow he may not be
With earth's bright revelry,
In love, in strife.

Yet, while abiding here,
He left with me good cheer,
Calmly he met the darkness and the end;

So on his tomb I lay
The wealth of yesterday,
That none may spend.

Henry Herbert Knibbs

HIS OWNE EPITAPH

Eternal rest on him bestowe,
  O Lord, and everlastynge light,
  Who lacked withal for sup or bite,
Shorn close on scalp and chin and browe,
Who was scrap't bare and smooth, I trowe
  As any turnip round, poor wighte:
Eternal rest on him bestowe.
Hard doome befell him here belowe,
  Drove forth and smote him in sore spite,
  Though "I appeal!" he cried with mighte,
A form of speech that 's playne enowe:
Eternal rest on him bestowe.

François Villon
Translated by Wilfrid Thorley

THE FLIGHT

Upon a cloud among the stars we stood:
The angel raised his hand, and looked, and said,
"Which world, of all yon starry myriad
Shall we make wing to?" The still solitude
Became a harp whereon his voice and mood
Made spheral music round his haloed head.
I spake — for then I had not long been dead —
"Let me look round upon the vasts, and brood
A moment on these orbs ere I decide. . . .

What is yon lower star that beauteous shines
And with soft splendor now incarnadines
Our wings? — There would I go and there abide."
Then he, as one who some child's thought divines:
"That is the world where yesternight you died."
Lloyd Mifflin

A QUESTION

See proud monuments of every shape and size,
Or deep in earth, or soaring to the skies,
Scattered profusely over Earth's broad crust,
Fair, hollow caskets holding naught but Dust.

'T is strange how hard Men strive
To keep alive,
In every age and under every clime,
The memory of the Dead;
Or from the gnawing tooth of Time,
Save the frail body, whence that Life has fled.

Is it Men feel that Death is something real?
Something that will endure, — and are they sure
That after Death's sharp pain they rest, —
Nor dream another Life's tumultuous Dream
        again?

If Man, instead of dying, at once flies
To happier worlds and fairer skies,
Why, then, proud monuments of every shape and
        size?
Why mournful sables and sad weeping eyes?
Elihu Vedder

THE SCEPTICS

It was the little leaves beside the road:

Said Grass, "What is that sound
So dismally profound,
That detonates and desolates the air?"
"That is St. Peter's bell,"
Said rain-wise Pimpernel;
"He is music to the godly,
Though to us he sounds so oddly,
And he terrifies the faithful unto prayer."

Then something very like a groan
Escaped the naughty little leaves.

Said Grass, "And whither track
These creatures all in black,
So woebegone and penitent and meek?"
"They're mortals bound for church,"
Said the little Silver Birch;
"They hope to get to heaven
And have their sins forgiven,
If they talk to God about it once a week."

And something very like a smile
Ran through the naughty little leaves.

Said Grass, "What is that noise
That startles and destroys
Our blessed summer — brooding when
          we're tired?"
"That's folk a-praising God,"
Said the tough old cynic Clod;

"They do it every Sunday,
They'll be all right on Monday;
It's just a little habit they've acquired."

And laughter spread among the little leaves.
Bliss Carman

"IO VICTIS"

I sing the hymn of the conquered, who fell in the
      Battle of Life, —
The hymn of the wounded, the beaten, who died
      overwhelmed in the strife;
Not the jubilant song of the victors, for whom the
      resounding acclaim
Of nations was lifted in chorus, whose brows wore
      the chaplet of fame, —
But the hymn of the low and the humble, the weary,
      the broken in heart,
Who strove and who failed, acting bravely a silent
      and desperate part;
Whose youth bore no flower on its branches, whose
      hopes burned in ashes away,
From whose hands slipped the prize they had
      grasped at, who stood at the dying of day
With the wreck of their life all around them, un-
      pitied, unheeded, alone,
With Death sweeping down o'er their failure, and
      all but their faith overthrown.

While the voice of the world shouts its chorus, —
      its pæan for those who have won;
While the trumpet is sounding triumphant, and
      high to the breeze and the sun

Glad banners are waving, hands clapping, and
    hurrying feet
Thronging after the laurel-crowned victors, I stand
    on the field of defeat —
In the shadow, with those who have fallen, and
    wounded, and dying, and there
Chant a requiem low, place my hand on their pain-
    knotted brows, breathe a prayer,
Hold the hand that is helpless, and whisper,
    "They only the victory win,
Who have fought the good fight, and have van-
    quished the demon that tempts us within;
Who have held to their faith unseduced by the
    prize that the world holds on high;
Who have dared for a high cause to suffer, resist,
    fight, — if need be, to die."

Speak, History! Who are Life's victors? Unroll
    thy long annals, and say,
Are they those whom the world called the victors —
    who won the success of a day?
The martyrs, or Nero? The Spartans who fell at
    Thermopylæ's tryst,
Or the Persians and Xerxes? His judges or Socra-
    tes? Pilate or Christ?

William Wetmore Story

VILLON'S REGRETS

*François Villon, being about to die, a worthy friar would
fain have shriven him, and did earnestly exhort him to
confess those acts of his life which he did regret. Villon
bade him return again when he might have had time to*

*bethink him of his sins. Upon the good father's return,
Villon was dead; but by his side were the following verses,
his last, wherein he set forth those things which he did
regret.*

I, FRANÇOIS VILLON, ta'en at last
To the rude bed where all must lie,
Fain would forget the turbid past
And lay me down in peace and die.
Would I be shrived? Ah — can I tell?
My sins but trifles seem to be,
Nor worth the dignity of Hell;
If not, then ill avails it me
To count them one and all — and yet —
There be some things which I regret!

The sack of abbeys, many a brawl,
A score of knife-thrusts in the dark,
Forced oft by Fate against the wall,
And years in prison, cold and stark —
These crimes and pains seem far away
Now that I come at length to die;
'T is idle for the Past to pray,
'T is hopeless for the Past to sigh;
These are a troubled dream — and yet
For them I have but scant regret!

The toil my mother had to know
What years I lay in gyves for debt;
A pretty song heard years ago,
When, I know not; where, I forget;
The crust I once kept for my own
(Though all too scant for my poor use);

The friend I left to die alone,
(Perdie! The watchmen pressed us close!)
Trifles against my crimes to set!
Yet these are all which I regret.

Captains and cutthroats not a few,
And maidens fair of many a clime
Have named me friend in the wild past
Whenas we wallowed in the slime;
Gamblers and rogues and clever thieves,
And unfrocked priests, a sorry crew —
(How stubbornly the memory cleaves
To all who have befriended you!)
I drain a cup to them, and yet —
Not these the friends whom I regret!

My foundered horse, who died for me
(Nor whip nor spur were his, I ween!)
That day the hangman looked to see
Poor Villon earth and sky between!
A mongrel cur who shared my lot
Three bitter winters on the Isle:
He held the rabble off, God wot!
One time I cheated in the deal.
'T was but an instant, but I fled
Down a vile alley known to me —
There in the garbage he lay dead;
The gamblers raged — but I was free!
Humble, poor brutes at best; and yet —
They are the friends whom I regret!

And once the lilies were a-blow
Through all the sunny fields of France;

I marked one whiter than the snow,
And would have gathered it, perchance,
Had not some trifle I forget,
A Bishop's loot, a cask of wine
Purloined from some auberge — a bet —
Distracted this wild head of mine;
A childish fancy this, and yet —
It is this thing which I regret.

Again, I rode through Picardy
What time the vine was in the bud;
A little maiden smiled on me,
I might have kissed her, an' I would!
I've known a thousand maidens since,
And many have been kind to me —
I've never seen one quite so fair
As she, that day in Picardy;
Ashes of roses these, and yet —
They are the things which I regret.

One perfect lily grew for me,
And blossomed on another's breast;
Others have clasped the little hands
Whose rosy palms I might have pressed:
So as I die, my wasted youth
Mocks my dim eyes and fading breath —
Still, I have lived! And having lived
That much is mine — I mock at Death.
I should confess, you say. But yet —
Only for Life have I regret!

L'ENVOI

O bubbles of the vanished wine
To which my lips were never set!

O lips that dimpled close to mine,
Whose ruddy warmth I never met!
Father, poor trifles these, and yet —
They are the things which I regret!

John D. Swain

A DEAD MARCH

Play me a march, low-toned and slow — a march
    for a silent tread,
Fit for the wandering feet of one who dreams of the
    silent dead,
Lonely, between the bones below and the souls that
    are overhead.

Here for a while they smiled and sang, alive in the
    interspace,
Here with the grass beneath the foot, and the stars
    above the face,
Now are their feet beneath the grass, and whither
    has flown their grace?

Who shall assure us whence they come, or tell us
    the way they go?
Verily, life with them was joy and, now they have
    left us, woe.
Once they were not, and now they are not, and this
    is the sum we know.

Orderly range the seasons due, and orderly roll the
    stars.
How shall we deem the soldier brave who frets of
    his wounds and scars?
Are we as senseless brutes that we should dash at
    the well-seen bars?

No, we are here, with feet unfixed, but ever as if
with lead,

Drawn from the orbs which shine above to the orb
on which we tread,

Down to the dust from which we came and with
which we shall mingle dead.

No, we are here to wait, and work, and strain our
banished eyes,

Weary and sick of soil and toil, and hungry and
fain for skies,

Far from the reach of wingless men, and not to be
scaled with cries.

No, we are here to bend our necks to the yoke of
tyrant Time,

Welcoming all the gifts he gives us — glories of
youth and prime,

Patiently watching them all depart as our heads
grow white as rime.

Why do we mourn the days that go — for the same
sun shines each day,

Ever a Spring her primrose hath, and ever a May
her may;

Sweet as the rose that died last year is the rose that
is born to-day.

Do we not, too, return, we men, as ever the round
earth whirls?

Never a head is dimmed with gray but another is
sunned with curls;

She was a girl and he was a boy, but yet there are
boys and girls.

Ah, but alas! for the smile of smiles that never but
    one face wore;
Ah, for the voice that has flown away like a bird to
    an unseen shore;
Ah, for the face — the flower of flowers — that
    blossoms on earth no more.

Cosmo Monkhouse

THE PIPES O' GORDON'S MEN

Home comes a lad with the bonny hair,
And the kilted plaid that the hill-clans wear;
And you hear the mother say:
"Whear ha' ye ben, wee Laddie; whear ha' ye ben
    th' day?"
"O! I ha' ben wi' Gordon's men;
Dinna ye hear th' bagpipes play?
And I followed th' soldiers across th' green,
And doon th' road tae Aberdeen.
And when I'm a mon, my Mither,
And th' Hielanders parade,
I'll be marchin' there, wi' my feyther's pipes,
And I'll wear th' red cockade."

Beneath the Soudan's sky ye ken the smoke,
As the clans reply when the tribesmen spoke.
Then the charge roars by!
The death-sweat clings to the kilted form that the
    stretcher brings,
And the iron-nerved surgeons say:
"Whear ha' ye ben, my Laddie; whear ha' ye ben
    th' day?"
"O, I ha' ben wi' Gordon's men;

Dinna ye hear th' bagpipes play?
An' I piped th' clans from the river barge
Across the sands, an' through the charge.
An' I — skirled — th' pibroch — keen — an' high,
But th' pipes — ben broke — an' — my — lips —
      ben — dry."

CORONACH

Upon the hill-side, high and steep,
Where rank on rank the soldiers sleep, —
Where the silent cannons beside the path,
Point the last forced-march that the soldier
          hath, —
Where the falling grave-grass has partly hid
The round-shot, heaped in a pyramid —
A white stone rises; across its face
You can read the words that the chisels trace:
"Whear ha' ye ben, wee Laddie; whear ha' ye
      ben th' day?"
"O, I ha' ben wi' Gordon's men;
Dinna ye hear th' bagpipes play?"

J. Scott Glasgow

AT THE TOP OF THE ROAD

"But, Lord," she said, "my shoulders still are
      strong —
I have been used to bear the load so long;

"And see, the hill is passed, and smooth the
      road . . ."
"Yet," said the Stranger, " yield me now thy
      load."

Gently he took it from her, and she stood
Straight-limbed and lithe, in new-found maiden-
        hood,

Amid long, sunlit fields; around them sprang
A tender breeze, and birds and rivers sang.

"My Lord," she said, "the land is very fair!"
Smiling, he answered: "Was it not so there?"

"There?" In her voice a wondering question lay:
"Was I not always here, then, as to-day?"

He turned to her with strange, deep eyes aflame:
" Knowest thou not this kingdom, nor my name?"

"Nay," she replied: "but this I understand —
That thou art Lord of Life in this dear land!"

*" Yea, child," he murmured, scarce above his
        breath:*
*"Lord of the Land! but men have named me
        Death."*

                    Charles Buxton Going

AFTERWARDS

I know that these poor rags of womanhood, —
This oaten pipe, whereon the wild winds played
Making sad music, — tattered and outfrayed,
Cast off, played out, — can hold no more of
        good,
Of love, or song, or sense of sun and shade.

What homely neighbors elbow me (hard by
'Neath the black yews) I know I shall not know,
Nor take account of changing winds that blow,
Shifting the golden arrow, set on high
On the gray spire, nor mark who come and go.

Yet would I lie in some familiar place,
Nor share my rest with uncongenial dead, —
Somewhere, maybe, where friendly feet will
     tread, —
As if from out some little chink of space
Mine eyes might see them tripping overhead.

And though too sweet to deck a sepulcher
Seem twinkling daisy-buds and meadow-grass;
And so would more than serve me, lest they pass
Who fain would know what woman rested there,
What her demeanor, or her story was, —

For these I would that on a sculptured stone
(Fenced 'round with iron work to keep secure)
Should sleep a form with folded palms demure,
In aspect like the dreamer that was gone,
With these words carved: *"I hoped, but was
     not sure."*

                             Violet Fane

WHEN SHE CAME TO GLORY

Nay, loose my hand and let me go!
God's glories pierce and frighten.
I want my house, my fires, my bread,
My sheets to wash and whiten.

I liked the dusty roads of earth,
The brambles and the roaming;
I liked the flowers that used to fade,
The small lamp in the gloaming.

The fields of God, they blind my eyes.
Dread is this heavenly tillage.
I want the sweet, lost homeliness
Of the door-yards of our village.

Where are the accustomed, common
        things —
The cups we drank together;
The old shoes that he laced for me,
The cape for rainy weather?

Dear were our stumbling, human ways,
His words' impetuous flurry,
His tossed hair, the kind, anxious brow,
His steps' too-eager hurry.

O tall archangel with such wings,
Your beauty is too burning!
Give me once more my threadbare dress
And the sound of his feet returning.
                    Florence Wilkinson Evans

HERACLITUS

They told me, Heraclitus, they told me you were
        dead,
They brought me bitter news to hear and bitter
        tears to shed.

I wept as I remember'd how often you and I
Had tired the sun with talking and sent him down
the sky.

And now that thou art lying, my dear old Carian
guest,
A handful of grey ashes, long, long ago at rest,
Still are thy pleasant voices, thy nightingales,
awake;
For Death, he taketh all away, but them he cannot
take.

William Johnson Cory

"'T IS ALL AND NOTHING"

Writ on a ruined palace in Kashmir:
"The end is nothing, and the end is near."

Where are the voices kings were glad to hear?
Where now the feast, the song, the bayadere?
The end is nothing, and the end is near.

And yonder lovely rose; alas! my dear!
See the November garden, rank and drear.
The end is nothing, and the end is near.

See! how the rain-drop mingles with the mere.
Mark! how the age devours each passing year.
The end is nothing, and the end is near.

Forms rise and grow and wane and disappear,
The life allotted thee is now and here: —
The end is nothing, and the end is near.

Then vex thyself no more with thought austere
Take what thou canst while thou abidest here.
Seek finer pleasures each returning year :—
The end is nothing, and the end is near.

. . .

Joy is the Lord, and Love His charioteer;
Be tranquil and rejoicing; oh, my dear!
Shun the wild seas, far from the breakers steer;
The end is Vision, and the end is near.

Ah! banish hope and doubt, regret and fear,
Check the gay laugh, but dry the idle tear.
Search! Is the light within thee burning clear?
The end is Vision and the end is near.

List to the wisdom learn'd of saint and seer!
The living Lord is joy, and peace His sphere;
Rebel no more! throw down thy shield and spear,
Surrender all thyself; true life is here ;
The end is Vision, and the end is near.

Forget not this, forget not that, my dear!
'T is all and nothing, and the end is near.

Anonymous

"HINC NOSTRÆ LACRIMÆ"

'T was ever so —
The young, the beautiful, the brave —
Are first to go!

The halt and blind
In all the days and ages gone
Remain behind!

They venture far
Who gird at fate and death to gain
The blazing star!

Yet shall they glow
In constellations vast, above
The earthly show!

So rest our tears
To nourish memories green
Through waiting years,

While in the sky
Shine they forever in the golden light
Who dared to die!

Don C. Seitz

BREAKING THE SILENCE

If I should fall asleep one day,
  All overworn,
And should my spirit from the clay
Go dreaming out the Heavenward way,
  Or thence be softly borne, —

I pray you, angels, do not first
  Assail mine ear
With that blest anthem oft rehearsed, —
"Behold the bonds of Death are burst," —
  Lest I should faint with fear.

But let some happy bird at hand
  The silence break:

So shall I dimly understand
That dawn has touched a blossoming land,
    And sigh myself awake.

From that deep rest emerging so
    To lift the head
And see the bath-flower's bell of snow, :
The pink Arbutus, and the low
    Spring-beauty streaked with red,

Will all suffice — no other where .
    Impelled to roam, —
Till some blithe wanderer, passing fair, :
Will smiling pause, of me aware,
    And murmur, "Welcome home!"

So, sweetly greeted, I shall rise
    To kiss her cheek;
Then lightly soar in lovely guise,
As one familiar with the skies,
    Who finds, and need not seek.

                        Amanda T. Jones

AT SUNSET

To all who went adventuring at the last,
And to new voyages at sunset passed,
Too brave at heart, too high of hope to see
Their sky horizoned by mortality:
Ossian who left the ease that age had earned
That he might win to where the Fenians burned;
And him who found new hopes invincible
Because the sea had something yet to tell;

And many another one who, scorning death,
Went forth enkindling with his latest breath
To glory and a never-dying flame,
The funeral pyre that lights a hero name: —
These lines I consecrate that they may aid
Me when I go upon that last crusade,
For though the West be grey and no light linger
Where beckoned once the sunset's flickering fin-
    ger,
No business of the earth will hold me back
From seeking out where they have found a track.
I will launch forth elate, and leave again
These little harbours and the ways of men,
And light again all that old Western fire
With the red sunset of my last desire.

Seumas O'Sullivan

THE DEPARTED FRIEND

He is not dead, this friend, not dead,
But in the path we mortals tread,
Got some few trifling steps ahead
    And nearer to the end, —
So that you, too, once past the bend
Shall meet again, as, face to face, this friend
    You fancy dead.

Push gaily on, strong heart, the while
You travel forward, mile by mile,
He loiters with a backward smile
    Till you can overtake, —
And strains his eyes to search his wake,
Or, whistling as he sees you through the break,
    Waits on a stile.

Though he that ever kind and true
Kept stoutly step by step with you
Your whole, long, gusty life-time through
    Be gone awhile before,
But now a moment gone before, —
Yet doubt not soon the seasons shall restore
    Your friend to you.

He has but turned a corner; still
He pushes on with right good will,
Through mire and marsh, through heugh and
    hill,
    That selfsame, arduous way,
That selfsame, upland, helpful way,
That you and he through many a doubtful day
    Attempted still.

Robert Louis Stevenson

UP-HILL

Does the road wind up-hill all the way?
    Yes, to the very end.
Will the day's journey take the whole long day?
    From morn to night, my friend.

But is there for the night a resting-place?
    A roof for when the slow, dark hours begin.
May not the darkness hide it from my face?
    You cannot miss that inn.

Shall I meet other wayfarers at night?
    Those who have gone before.
Then must I knock, or call when just in sight?
    They will not keep you waiting at that door.

Shall I find comfort, travel-sore and weak?
   Of labor you shall find the sum.
Will there be beds for me and all who seek?
   Yea, beds for all who come.
               Christina Georgina Rossetti

WITH THE TIDE

(Written on the day after Theodore Roosevelt's death)

Somewhere I read, in an old book whose name
Is gone from me, I read that when the days
Of a man are counted, and his business done,
There comes up the shore at evening, with the tide,
To the place where he sits, a boat —
And in the boat, from the place where he sits, he
     sees,
Dim in the dusk, dim and yet so familiar,
The faces of his friends long dead; and knows
They come for him, brought in upon the tide,
To take him where men go at set of day.
Then rising, with his hands in theirs, he goes
Between them his last steps, that are the first
Of the new life — and with the ebb they pass,
Their shaken sail grown small upon the moon.

Often I thought of this, and pictured me
How many a man who lives with throngs about
     him,
Yet straining through the twilight for that boat,
Shall scarce make out one figure in the stern,
And that so faint, its features shall perplex him
With doubtful memories, and his heart hang back.

But others, rising as they see the sail
Increase upon the sunset, hasten down,
Hands out and eyes elated; for they see,
Head over head, crowding from bow to stern,
Re-peopling their long loneliness with smiles,
The faces of their friends; and such go forth
Content upon the ebb tide, with safe hearts.

But never
To worker summoned when his day was done
Did mounting tide bring in such freight of friends
As stole to you up the white wintry shingle,
That night while they that watched you thought you
      slept.
Softly they came, and beached the boat, and gath-
      ered
In the still cove under the icy stars,
Your last-born, and the dear loves of your heart,
And all men that have loved right more than ease,
And honour above honours; all who gave
Free-handed of their best for other men,
And thought their giving taking, they who knew
Man's natural state is effort, up and up —
All these were there, so great a company
Perchance you marvelled, wondering what great
      ship
Had brought that throng unnumbered to the cove
Where the boys used to beach their light canoe
After old happy picnics —

But these, your friends and children, to whose
      hands
Committed, in the silent night you rose

And took your last faint steps —
These led you down, O great American,
Down to the winter night and the white beach,
And there you saw that the huge hull that
     waited
Was not as are the boats of the other dead,
Frail craft for a brief passage; no, for this
Was first of a long line of towering transports,
Storm-worn and ocean-weary every one,
The ships you launched, the ships you manned,
     the ships
That now, returning from their sacred quest
With the thrice-sacred burden of their dead,
Lay waiting there to take you forth with them,
Out with the ebb tide, on some farther quest.

               Edith Wharton

THE GREAT ADVENTURE

God, the Master Pilot —
  Or Gods, if such there be —
Pour me no weakling's measure
  When ye pour the wine for me,
Of pain, of love, of pleasure —
  I'll drain the draught ye give;
Of good and ill, give me the fill
  Of the life ye bade me live.

Spare me no tithe of favor,
  With fortune pave my path,
Nor hold the hand of vengeance
  When I deserve your wrath.

Whatever fates ye send me,
　　Whatever cast the sky,
Grant me the grace to live a man,
　　And as a man to die.

Upon the good I render
　　Let shine your proudest sun,
And rest me in the valleys
　　When my last trick is done.
For these, your utmost portions,
　　I'll pay the utmost toll,
So this, my life, becomes the great
　　Adventure of my Soul.
　　　　　　　Major Kendall Banning

WHEN I HAVE GONE WEIRD WAYS

When I have finished with this episode,
Left the hard, up-hill road,
And gone weird ways to seek another load —
　　O, friends, regret me not, nor weep for me,
　　Child of Infinity.

Nor dig a grave, nor rear for me a tomb
To say with lying writ: "Here in the gloom,
He who loved bigness takes a narrow room,
　　Content to pillow here his weary head,
　　For he is dead."

But give my body to the funeral pyre,
And bid the laughing fire,
Eager and strong and swift, like my desire,
　　Scatter my subtle essence into space —
　　Free me of time and place.

And sweep the bitter ashes from the hearth,
Fling back the dust I borrowed from the earth
Into the chemic broil of death and birth:
　　The vast alembic of the cryptic scheme,
　　Warm with the master-dream.

And thus, — O little house that sheltered me,
Dissolve again in wind and rain, to be
Part of the cosmic weird economy.
And O! how oft with new life shalt thou lift
　　Out of the atom-drift!

John G. Neihardt

ROOM FOR A SOLDIER!

Room for a soldier! Lay him in the clover,
He loved the fields and they shall be his cover:
Make his mound with hers who called him once
　　her lover:
　　Where the rain may rain upon it,
　　Where the sun may shine upon it,
　　Where the lamb hath lain upon it,
　　And the bee will dine upon it.

Bear him to no dismal tomb under city churches;
Take him to the fragrant fields, by the silver
　　birches,
Where the whippoorwill shall mourn, where the
　　oriole perches:
　　Make his mound with sunshine on it,
　　Where the bee will dine upon it,
　　Where the lamb hath lain upon it,
　　And the rain will rain upon it.

Busy as the busy bee, his rest should be the clover;
Gentle as a lamb was he, and the fern should be his
      cover;
Fern and rosemary shall grow my soldier's pillow
      over:
    Where the rain may rain upon it,
    Where the sun may shine upon it,
    Where the lamb hath lain upon it,
    And the bee will dine upon it.

Sunshine in his heart, the rain would come full
      often
Out of those tender eyes which ever more did
      soften:
He never could look cold till we saw him in his cof-
      fin.
    Make his mound with sunshine on it,
    Where the wind may sigh upon it,
    Where the moon may stream upon it,
    And Memory shall dream upon it.

"Captain" or "Colonel" — whatever invocation
Suit our hymn the best, no matter for thy station, —
On thy grave the rain shall fall from the eyes of a
      mighty nation!
    Long as the sun doth shine upon it,
    Shall glow the goodly pine upon it;
    Long as the stars do gleam upon it
    Shall Memory come to dream upon it.

               Thomas William Parsons

THE END OF ALL

Blest are the dormant⁷
In death: they repose
From bondage and torment,
From passions and woes,
From the yoke of the world and the snares of
　　　the traitor.
The grave, the grave is the true liberator.

Griefs chase one another
Around the earth's dome:
In the arms of the mother
Alone is our home.
Woo pleasures, ye triflers! The thoughtful are
　　　wiser;
The grave, the grave is their one tranquillizer.

Is the good man unfriended
On life's ocean-path?
Where storms have expended
Their turbulent wrath?
Are his labors requited by slander and rancor?
The grave, the grave is his sure bower-anchor.

To gaze on the faces
Of lost ones anew,
To lock in embraces
The loved and the true,
Were a rapture to make even Paradise brighter.
The grave, the grave is the great reuniter.

Crown the corpse then with laurels,
The conqueror's wreath,

Make joyous with carols
The chamber of death,
And welcome the victor with cymbal and psalter :
The grave, the grave is the only exalter.

James Clarence Mangan

THE DANCE OF DEATH

He is the despots' Despot. All must bide,
Later or soon, the message of his might;
Princes and potentates their heads must hide,
Touched by the awful sigil of his right;
Beside the Kaiser he at eve doth wait
And pours a potion in his cup of state;
The stately Queen his bidding must obey;
No keen-eyed Cardinal shall him affray;
And to the Dame that wantoneth he saith —
"Let be, Sweet-heart, to junket and to play."
There is no King more terrible than Death.

The lusty Lord, rejoicing in his pride,
He draweth down; before the armèd Knight
With jingling bridle-rein he still doth ride;
He crosseth the strong Captain in the fight;
The Burgher, grave, he beckons from debate;
He hales the Abbot by his shaven pate,
Nor for the Abbess' wailing will delay;
No bawling Mendicant shall say him nay;
E'en to the pyx the Priest he followeth,
Nor can the Leech his chilling finger stay . . .
There is no King more terrible than Death.

All things must bow to him. And woe betide
The Wine-bibber, — the Roisterer by night;

Him the feast-master, many bouts defied,
Him 'twixt the pledging and the cup shall smite;
Woe to the Lender at usurious rate,
The hard Rich Man, the hireling Advocate;
Woe to the Judge that selleth Law for pay;
Woe to the Thief that like a beast of prey
With creeping tread the traveller harryeth: —
These, in their sin, the sudden sword shall slay . . .
There is no King more terrible than Death.

He hath no pity, — nor will be denied.
When the low hearth is garnishèd and bright,
Grimly he flingeth the dim portal wide,
And steals the Infant in the Mother's sight;
He hath no pity for the scorned of fate: —
He spares not Lazarus lying at the gate,
Nay, nor the Blind that stumbleth as he may;
Nay, the tired Ploughman, — at the sinking ray, —
In the last furrow, — feels an icy breath,
And knows a hand hath turned the team astray . . .
There is no King more terrible than Death.

He hath no pity. For the new-made Bride,
Blithe with the promise of her life's delight,
That wanders gladly by her Husband's side,
He with the clatter of his drum doth fright;
He scares the Virgin at the convent grate;
The Maid half-won, the Lover passionate;
He hath no grace for weakness and decay:
The tender Wife, the Widow bent and gray,
The feeble Sire whose footstep faltereth, —
All these he leadeth by the lonely way . . .
There is no King more terrible than Death.

ENVOY

Youth, for whose ear and monishing of late,
I sang of Prodigals and lost estate,
Have thou thy joy of living and be gay;
But know not less that there must come a
     day —
Aye, and perchance e'en now it hasteneth, —
When thine own heart shall speak to thee
     and say, —
There is no King more terrible than Death.

Austin Dobson

MAN'S GUESS

Far beyond Man's utmost sight
His daring mind pursues its flight.
Yet ever ends where it began — in Night.

The clear eyes of the wisest Sage,
The firm faith of the greatest Saint;
One comes to where his Eyes grow dim,
The other where his Faith grows faint.

Scheme after scheme he vainly tries,
Star after star he sees arise,
And far beyond them in his fancy flies,
Ever returning with this vague surmise
To which he clings even in darkest night,
'T is but a guess, —

     "All things may turn out right."

Elihu Vedder

MY OLD COUNSELOR

The Sun looked from his everlasting skies,
He laughed into my daily-dying eyes;
He said to me, the brutal shining Sun:
"Poor, fretful, hot, rebellious little one!

"Thou shalt not find it, yet there shall be truth;
Thou shalt grow old, but yet there shall be youth;
Thou shalt not do, yet great deeds shall be done, —
Believe me, child, I am an old, old Sun!

"Thou mayst go blind, yet fair will bloom the
        spring;
Thou mayst not hear them, but the birds will sing;
Thou mayst despair, no less will hope be rife;
Thou must lie dead, but many will have life.

"Thou mayst declare of love: it is a dream!
Yet long with love, my love, the Earth will teem:
Let not thy foolish heart be borne so low, —
Lift up thy heart! Exult that it is so!"

Gertrude Hall

THE PAINTING

There is a painting on my wall,
A blue daub of the sea,
With a black rock lifting tall
And a gray haze over all,
And the wind in a bended tree.
It is a window where my soul goes free!

Dusk after dusk I come into that room
From the won fields of life,
From the weary human strife,
And see my painting like a pleasant bloom,
Against the white wall there,
And know God meant His kingdoms to be fair.

The towers and the streets grow blurred and dim,
I see the world once more
As it occurred to Him,
The clean sea and the clasping shore,
And the wind's hand shaking music from a tree!
That is the living universe to me;
The rest becomes a painted masque of days
Wherein I build at golden make-believe,
For purses and for praise,
And put a solemn face upon it all
My childish fellow builders to deceive.
But here upon my study-wall
Hangs the blue gate to wide reality,
The strong rock, and the singing tree,
And the shore asleep in the water's arm,
Like a woman taken for her charm,
Clasped by that lover of all lands, the sea!

Impoverished is the Man who owns one world,
And one alone, whose soul has never trod
The bold beginnings of the path to God,
Who goes with ne'er a flaming dream unfurled
Along the crawling highways of his kind,
Clinging to vapors and to husks
With futile hands, half lost and wholly blind,
Fearful of shadows, yet without the mind
To see what stars may fleck his journey's dusks.

To him be pity! For his soul shall grope
In vain for Beauty and for Hope.

Oh, that a window such as mine
Might swing in every wall!
With the black rock lifting tall
And the wind like sweet, untasted wine,
And the blown tree,
And the shore and the sea!

Dana Burnet

PASSAGE TO INDIA

Singing my days!
Singing the great achievements of the present,
The past — the infinite greatness of the past!

Passage to India!
Lo, soul, seest thou not God's purpose from the first?
The earth to be spann'd, connected by network,
The races, neighbours, to marry and be given in
      marriage,
The oceans to be cross'd, the distant brought near,
The lands to be welded together.

A worship new I sing,
You captains, voyagers, explorers, yours,
You engineers, you architects, machinists, yours,
You, not for trade or transportation only,
But in God's name, and for thy sake O soul.

Ah more than any priest, O soul, we too believe in
      God,
But with the mystery of God we dare not dally.

O soul thou pleasest me, I thee,
Sailing these seas or on the hills, or waking in the
    night,
Thoughts, silent thoughts, of Time and Space and
    Death, like waters flowing,
Bear me indeed as through the regions infinite,
Whose air I breathe, whose ripples hear, lave me
    all over.
Bathe me O God in thee, mounting to thee,
I and my soul to range in range of thee.

O Thou transcendent!
Nameless, the fibre and the breath,
Light of the light, shedding forth universes, thou
    centre of them,
Thou mightier centre of the true, the good, the
    loving.

Thou moral, spiritual fountain — affection's source
    — thou reservoir!
(O pensive soul of me — O thirst unsatisfied —
    waitest not there —
Waitest not haply for us somewhere there the Com-
    rade perfect?)
Thou pulse — thou motive of the stars, suns, sys-
    tems,
That circling, move in order, safe, harmonious,
Athwart the shapeless vastnesses of space!
How should I think, how breathe a single breath,
    how speak, if, out of myself,
I could not launch, to those, superior universes?

Swiftly I shrivel at the thought of God,

At Nature and its wonders, Time and Space and
      Death,
But that I, turning, call to thee, O soul, thou actual
      Me —
And lo, thou gently masterest the orbs,
Thou matest Time, smilest content at Death,
And fillest, swellest full the vastnesses of Space.

Passage! Immediate passage! The blood burns in
      my veins!
Away O soul! Hoist instantly the anchor!
Cut the hawsers — haul out — shake out every sail!
Have we not stood here like trees in the ground
      long enough?
Have we not grovel'd here long enough, eating and
      drinking like mere brutes?
Have we not darken'd and dazed ourselves with
      books long enough?

Sail forth — steer for the deep waters only!
Reckless O soul, exploring, I with thee, and thou
      with me,
For we are bound where mariner has not yet dared
      to go,
And we will risk the ship, ourselves and all.

O my brave soul!
O farther farther sail!
O daring joy, but safe! are they not all the seas of
      God?
O farther, farther, farther sail!
                       Walt Whitman

RELIGION

Creeds change,
All outward forms
Recast themselves.
Sacred groves, temples and churches
Rise and rot and fall.
Races and nations
And the various tongues of men
Come and go and are
Recorded, numbered
And forgotten in the repetition
And the drift
Of many ages.
All outward circumstances
May be different
But there lives no man —
Nor ever lived one —
Who, in the silence of his heart,
Feeling his need,
Has not cried out,
Shaping some prayer
To the unchanging God.

Paul Kester

PRAYER AMID FLAMES

Holy Spirit, I cry to thee.
Fire and Victor-Song is thy name.
Shine in our need, oh spirit of power,
Shine o'er the gulf of our dread last hour,
Burn into ashes our mortal frame! —

Even in death mine arms shall be
Outstretched in prayer to thy deathless flame.
From the Swedish of Verner von Heidenstam
(Translated by Charles Wharton Stork)

"GATHER US IN"

Rend each man's temple veil and bid it fall,
  Gather our rival faiths within thy fold!
Gather us in, Thou Love that fillest all!
  That we may know that Thou hast been of old —
    Gather us in!

Gather us in! We worship only Thee;
  In varied names we stretch a common hand;
In diverse forms a common soul we see;
  In many ships we seek one spirit-land —
    Gather us in!

Each sees one color of Thy rainbow light,
  Each looks upon one tint and calls it heaven;
Thou art the fulness of our partial sight;
  We are not perfect till we find the seven —
    Gather us in!

Thine is the mystic light great India craves,
  Thine is the Parsee's sin-destroying beam,
Thine is the Buddhist's rest from tossing waves,
  Thine is the empire of vast China's dream —
    Gather us in!

Thine is the Roman's strength without his pride,
  Thine is the Greek's glad world without its
    graves,

Thine is Judea's law with love beside,
  The truth that centers and the grace that
    saves —
          Gather us in!

Some seek a Father in the heavens above,
  Some ask a human image to adore,
Some crave a spirit vast as life and love:
  Within Thy mansions we have all and more —
          Gather us in!
                              George Matheson

DAWN IN THE DESERT

When the first opal presage of the morn
Quickened the east, the good Merwan arose,
And by his open tent-door knelt and prayed.

Now in that pilgrim caravan was one
Whose heart was heavy with dumb doubts, whose
      eyes
Drew little balm from slumber. Up and down
Night-long he paced the avenues of sand
'Twixt tent and tent, and heard the jackals
      snarl,
The camels moan for water. This one came
On Merwan praying, and to him outcried —
(The tortured spirit bursting its sealed fount
As doth the brook on Damavend in spring)
"How knowest thou that any Allah is?"
Swift from the sand did Merwan lift his face,
Flung toward the east an arm of knotted bronze,
And said, as upward shot a shaft of gold:

"Dost need a torch to show to thee the dawn?"
Then prayed again.

        When on the desert's rim
In sudden awful splendor stood the sun,
Through all that caravan there was no knee
But bowed to Allah.

             Clinton Scollard

IMMORTALITY

Two caterpillars crawling on a leaf,
  By some strange accident in contact came;
Their conversation, passing all belief,
  Was that same argument, the very same,
That has been "proed and conned," from man to
      man;
Yea, ever since this wondrous world began.
      The ugly creatures,
        Deaf and dumb and blind,
       Devoid of features
        That adorn mankind,
Were vain enough, in dull and worldly strife,
To speculate upon a future life.
  The first was optimistic, full of hope —
  The second, quite dyspeptic, seemed to mope.
Said number one, "I'm sure of our salvation."
Said number two, "I'm sure of our damnation.
  Our ugly forms alone would seal our fates,
  And bar our entrance through the golden gates.
Suppose that death should take us unawares,
How could we ever climb the golden stairs?
  If maidens shun us as they pass us by,
  Would angels bid us welcome to the sky?

I wonder what great crimes we have committed,
That leave us so forlorn, so unpitied?
    Perhaps we've been ungrateful, unforgiving,
    'T is plain to me life is not worth the living."
"Come, come, cheer up," the jovial one replied —
"Let's take a look upon the other side:
    Suppose we cannot fly like moths and millers,
    Are we to blame for being caterpillars?
Will that same God that doomed us crawl the earth,
A prey to every bird that's given birth,
    Forgive our captor as he eats and sings,
    And damn poor us because we have no wings?
If we can't skim the air, like owl or bat,
The worm will turn for a' that."
    They argued through the Summer — Autumn
        nigh;
    The ugly things composed themselves to die —
And so, to make their funeral quite complete,
Each wrapped him in his little winding-sheet.
    The tangled web encompassed them full soon —
    Each for his coffin made him a cocoon.
All through the Winter's chilling blasts they lay,
Dead to the world, aye, dead as any human clay.
    Lo! Spring comes forth with all her warmth and
        love;
    She brings sweet justice from the realms
        above —
She breaks the chrysalis — she resurrects the
    dead —
Two butterflies ascend, encircling her head.
    And so, this emblem shall forever be
    A sign of Immortality.

                                Joseph Jefferson

THE WISH

The wish, that of the living whole
   No life may fail beyond the grave,
   Derives it not from what we have
The likest God within the soul?

Are God and Nature then at strife,
   That Nature lends such evil dreams?
   So careful of the type she seems,
So careless of the single life

That I, considering everywhere
   Her secret meaning in her deeds,
   And finding that of fifty seeds
She often brings but one to bear —

I falter where I firmly trod,
   And falling with my weight of cares
   Upon the great world's altar-stairs
That slope thro' darkness up to God —

I stretch lame hands of faith, and grope,
   And gather dust and chaff, and call
   To what I feel is Lord of all,
And faintly trust the larger hope.

                      Tennyson

"NO COWARD SOUL IS MINE"

No coward soul is mine,
No trembler in the world's storm-troubled sphere:
   I see Heaven's glories shine,
And faith shines equal, arming me from fear.

O God within my breast,
Almighty, ever-present Deity!
    Life — that in me has rest,
As I — undying Life — have power in Thee!

    Vain are the thousand creeds
That move men's hearts: unutterably vain;
    Worthless as wither'd weeds,
Or idlest froth amid the boundless main,

    To waken doubt in one
Holding so fast by Thine infinity;
    So surely anchor'd on
The steadfast rock of Immortality.

    With wide-embracing love
Thy Spirit animates eternal years,
    Pervades and broods above,
Changes, sustains, dissolves, creates and rears.

    Though earth and man were gone,
And suns and universes cease to be,
    And Thou were left alone —
Every existence would exist in Thee.

    There is not room for Death,
Nor atom that his might could render void:
    Thou — Thou art Being and Breath,
And what Thou art may never be destroyed.

Emily Brontë

THE SECOND CRUCIFIXION

Loud mockers in the roaring street
  Say Christ is crucified again:
Twice pierced His gospel-bearing feet,
  Twice broken His great heart in vain.

I hear, and to myself I smile,
For Christ talks with me all the while.

No angel now to roll the stone
  From off His unawaking sleep,
In vain shall Mary watch alone,
  In vain the soldiers vigil keep.

Yet while they deem my Lord is dead
My eyes are on His shining head.

Ah! never more shall Mary hear
  That voice exceeding sweet and low
Within the garden calling clear:
  Her Lord is gone, and she must go.

Yet all the while my Lord I meet
In every London lane and street.

Poor Lazarus shall wait in vain,
  And Bartimeus still go blind;
The healing hem shall ne'er again
  Be touch'd by suffering humankind.

Yet all the while I see them rest,
The poor and outcast, on His breast.

No more unto the stubborn heart
　　With gentle knocking shall He plead,
No more the mystic pity start,
　　For Christ twice dead is dead indeed:

So in the street I hear men say —
Yet Christ is with me all the day.
　　　　　　　　　　Richard Le Gallienne

A CONCLUSION

If all the dream-like things are vain,
If all the strange delight and pain
　　Of love and beauty cannot be
　　The heirs of immortality, —
Then shall I worship all the more
Those images I now adore.
　　If all things perish, it were best
　　To die with beauty, — lie at rest
In her great drift of ruined roses,
With lovely songs to have our closes, —
　　Yea, as on some transcendent pyre
　　Of sandalwood, to pass in fire
'Mid broken alabaster, whence
Arise great clouds of frankincense,
　　Carved ivory and sard, and robes
　　Of purple dye, and magic globes
Of burning crystal, scattered gems
Like flowers, and holy diadems,
　　Papyrus writ with perfect rimes,
　　And lutes fulfilled of tender chimes,
And lucid cups all scriptured round
With slim, white, dancing gods vine-bound,

And agate lamps, whence tongues of light
Flare out into the endless night.

Rachel Annand Taylor

TEARS

When I consider Life and its few years —
A wisp of fog betwixt us and the sun;
A call to battle, and the battle done
Ere the last echo dies within our ears;
A rose choked in the grass; an hour of fears;
The gusts that past a darkening shore do beat;
The burst of music down an unlistening street —
I wonder at the idleness of tears.
Ye old, old dead, and ye of yesternight,
Chieftains, and bards, and keepers of the sheep,
By every cup of sorrow that ye had,
Loose me from tears, and make me see aright
How each hath back what once he stayed to weep:
Homer his sight, David his little lad!

Lizette Woodworth Reese

THE WASHERWOMAN'S SONG

In a very humble cot,
In a rather quiet spot,
In the suds and in the soap,
Worked a woman full of hope;
Working, singing, all alone,
In a sort of undertone:
"With the Savior for a friend,
He will keep me to the end."

Sometimes happening along,
I had heard the semi-song,
   And I often used to smile,
   More in sympathy than guile;
But I never said a word
In regard to what I heard,
   As she sang about her friend
   Who would keep her to the end.

Not in sorrow nor in glee
Working all day long was she,
   As her children, three or four,
   Played around her on the floor;
But in monotones the song
She was humming all day long:
   "With the Savior for a friend,
   He will keep me to the end."

It's a song I do not sing,
For I scarce believe a thing
   Of the stories that are told
   Of the miracles of old;
But I know that her belief
Is the anodyne of grief,
   And will always be a friend
   That will keep her to the end.

Just a trifle lonesome she,
Just as poor as poor could be;
   But her spirits always rose,
   Like the bubbles in the clothes,
And, though widowed and alone,
Cheered her with the monotone,

Of a Savior and a friend
Who would keep her to the end.

I have seen her rub and scrub,
On the washboard in the tub,
   While the baby, sopped in suds,
   Rolled and tumbled in the duds;
Or was paddling in the pools,
With old scissors stuck in spools;
   She still humming of her friend
   Who would keep her to the end.

Human hopes and human creeds
Have their root in human needs;
   And I should not wish to strip
   From that washerwoman's lip
Any song that she can sing,
Any hope that songs can bring;
   For the woman has a friend
   Who will keep her to the end.
Eugene F. Ware

" WITH WHOM IS NO VARIABLENESS, NEITHER SHADOW OF TURNING"

It fortifies my soul to know
That though I perish — Truth is so:
That howsoe'er I stray and range —
Whate'er I do, Thou dost not change.
I steadier step when I recall
That, if I slip, Thou dost not fall.
Arthur Hugh Clough

PIPPA'S SONG

The year's at the spring
And day's at the morn;
Morning's at seven;
The hillside's dew-pearled;
The lark's on the wing;
The snail's on the thorn:
God's in His heaven —
All's right with the world!

Robert Browning

CLEANTHES' HYMN

Lead thou me, God, Law, Reason, Motion, Life,
All names for Thee alike are vain and hollow:
Lead me, for I will follow without strife,
Or — if I strive, still must I blindly follow!

Cleanthes the Stoic

PRAYER OF A POET TO GOD

Have mercy, Thou, upon my soul,
  Unclean against Thy flaming skies,
Unchaste beside Thy golden stole,
  Have mercy Thou! Let me arise
Before Thy throne in perfect peace,
Be pitiful, my soul release!

I know that all my days have been
  Misspent in paths afar from Thee;
I know mine eyes have quickly seen
  The things Thou wouldst not have me see,
That through the thoughtless years I saw
Uncounted scenes, but not Thy law.

Forgive the lies my tongue exclaimed,
   The heedless truths that slew the weak,
Forgive the many faults I blamed,
   Not on myself, but on the meek,
Forgive, Divine and Gracious God,
The buds I broke upon Thy sod!

Amazing is Thy mercy, Lord!
   Therefore remember not the times
My kisses, like a poisoned sword,
   Killed innocence, awakened crimes;
Forgive my passions uncontrolled,
The years I wandered from Thy fold!

My life on scarlet seas was tost,
   I swore to scorn Thy gift of grace,
I gloried Thou shouldst deem me lost —
   Perhaps I met Thee face to face?
Perhaps Thy wings refreshed my brow
The while I sealed with Vice a vow?

I stood on mounts and sang a song
   In praise of those that hate Thy name,
With laughing lips I did a wrong
   That shamed the very face of Shame.
Thrice blessed be Thy pity, God,
Else I should die beneath Thy rod!

Thou gavest me a singing voice
   To fill the earth with loveliness;
But I — it made my soul rejoice
   To make Thy children love Thee less,
Thy charity is boundless wide,
Forget, O Lord, my evil pride!

Have mercy, Thou, upon my soul
  Unclean against Thy stainless skies,
Unchaste beside Thy golden stole,
  Have mercy, Thou! My streaming eyes
Reveal what hells lay in my heart
The age I stood from Thee apart.

Joseph Bernard Rethy

EXILE FROM GOD

I do not fear to lay my body down
    In death, to share
The life of the dark earth and lose my own,
    If God is there.

I have so loved all sense of Him, sweet might
    Of color and sound, —
His tangible loveliness and living light
    That robes me 'round.

If to His heart in the hushed grave and dim
    We sink more near,
It shall be well — living we rest in Him.
    Only I fear

Lest from my God in lonely death I lapse,
    And the dumb clod
Lose Him, — for God is life, and death, perhaps,
    Exile from God.

John Hall Wheelock

PASSING OF OLD TRINITY

(Demolished seventy years ago)

Farewell! Farewell! They're falling fast,
  Pillar and arch and architrave;
Yon aged pile, to me the last
Sole record of the by-gone past,
  Is speeding to its grave:
And thoughts from memory's fountain flow,
  (As one by one, like wedded hearts,
  Each rude and mouldering stone departs,)
Of boyhood's happiness and woe, —
  Its sunshine and its shade:
And though each ray of early gladness
Comes mingled with the hues of sadness,
  I would not bid them fade.
They come, as come the stars at night, —
Like fountains gushing into light —
And close around my heart they twine,
Like ivy round the mountain pine!
Yes, they are gone — the sunlight smiles
All day upon its foot-worn aisles;
Those foot-worn aisles, where oft have trod
The humble worshipers of God,
In times long past, when Freedom first
From all the land in glory burst!

The heroic few! From him whose sword
  Was wielded in his country's cause,
To him who battled with his word,
  The bold expounder of her laws!
And they are gone — gone like the lone
  Forgotten echoes of their tread;

And from their niches now are gone
   The sculptured records of the dead!
As now I gaze, my heart is stirred
   With music of another sphere!
A low, sweet chime, which once was heard,
Comes like the note of some wild bird
   Upon my listening ear —
Recalling many a happy hour,
Reviving many a withered flower,
Whose bloom and beauty long have laid
Within my sad heart's silent shade:
Life's morning flowers! that bud and blow
   And wither ere the sun hath kissed
The dewdrops from their breasts of snow,
   Or dried the landscape's veil of mist!

Yes! When that sweetly mingled chime
Stole on my ear in boyhood's time,
My glad heart drank the thrilling joy,
   Undreaming of its future pains —
As spell-bound as the Theban boy
   Listening to Memnon's fabled strains!

Farewell, old fane! And though, unsung
   By bards thy many glories fell,
Though babbling fame had never rung
   Thy praises on his echoing bell —
Who that hath seen, can e'er forget
   Thy grey old spire? — Who that hath knelt
   Within thy sacred aisles, nor felt
Religion's self grow sweeter yet?

Yes! Though the decking hand of Time
   Glory to Greece's fanes hath given,

That, from her old heroic clime,
    Point proudly to their native heaven;
Though Rome hath many a ruined pile
    To speak the glory of her land,
And fair, by Egypt's sacred Nile,
    Her mouldering monuments may stand:
The joy that swells the gazer's heart,
    The pride that sparkles in his eye,
When pondering on these piles where art
    In crumbling majesty doth lie —
Ne'er blended with them keener joy
Than mine, when but a thoughtless boy
I gazed with awe-struck, wondering eye,
On thy old spire, my Trinity!
And thou shalt live like words of truth, —
Like golden monuments of youth —
As on the lake's unrippled breast
The mirrored mountain lies at rest,
So shalt thou lie, till life depart,
Mirrored for ages on my heart!

                                    Anonymous

"MINE THE LIGHT OF SETTING SUN"

"The haggard sky, the surf's dull roar,
The midnight storm are mine no more;
But mine the light of setting sun —
The call of birds when day is done;
The last sad gleam is loth to pass,
It weeps upon the golden grass;
The sigh of leaves in evening air,
The distant bell that calls to prayer
And nothing from my spirit bars
The benediction of the stars."

                                    William Winter

THE LIGHT OF THE WORLD

It singeth low in every heart,
    We hear it each and all —
A song of those who answer not,
    However we may call.
They throng the silence of the breast;
    We see them as of yore —
The kind, the true, the brave, the sweet,
    Who walk with us no more.

More homelike seems the vast unknown,
    Since they have entered there;
To follow them were not so hard,
    Wherever they may fare.
They cannot be where God is not,
    On any sea or shore;
Whate'er betides, thy love abides,
    Our God for evermore!

                    Rev. John W. Chadwick

"THERE IS NO DEATH"

There is no death! The stars go down
    To rise upon some fairer shore,
And bright in heaven's jeweled crown
    They shine for evermore.

There is no death! The dust we tread
    Shall change beneath the summer showers
To golden grain or mellow fruit
    Or rainbow-tinted flowers.

The granite rocks disorganize
  To feed the hungry moss they bear;
The forest leaves drink daily life
  From out the viewless air.

There is no death! The leaves may fall,
  The flowers may fade and pass away —
They only wait, through wintry hours,
  The coming of the May.

There is no death! An angel form
  Walks o'er the earth with silent tread;
He bears our best loved things away,
  And then we call them "dead."

He leaves our hearts all desolate —
  He plucks our fairest, sweetest flowers;
Transplanted into bliss, they now
  Adorn immortal bowers.

The bird-like voice, whose joyous tones
  Made glad this scene of sin and strife,
Sings now an everlasting song,
  Around the tree of life.

Where'er He sees a smile too bright,
  Or heart too pure for taint and vice,
He bears it to that world of light,
  To dwell in Paradise.

Born unto that undying life,
  They leave us but to come again;
With joy to welcome them — the same
  Except in sin and pain.

And ever near us, though unseen,
  The dear immortal spirits tread;
For all the boundless Universe
  Is life — there are no dead.
                    John L. McCreery

BEYOND

When youthful faith hath fled —
  Of loving take thy leave;
Be constant to the dead —
  The dead cannot deceive.

Sweet, modest flowers of Spring,
  How fleet your balmy day!
And man's brief year can bring
  No secondary May:

No earthly burst again
  Of gladness out of gloom,
Fond hope and vision vain —
  Ungrateful to the tomb.

But 't is an old belief
  That on some solemn shore,
Beyond the sphere of grief,
  Dear friends shall meet once more;

— Beyond the sphere of Time,
  And Sin and Fate's control,
Serene in endless prime
  Of body and of soul.

That creed I fain would keep,
   That hope I'll not forego;
Eternal be the sleep,
   Unless to waken so.
                    John Gibson Lockhart

SONG OF THE UNIVERSAL

Come said the Muse,
Sing me a song no poet yet has chanted,
Sing me the universal.

In this broad earth of ours,
Amid the measureless grossness and the slag,
Enclosed and safe within its central heart,
Nestles the seed perfection.
                 •   •   •

And thou America,
For the scheme's culmination, its thought and its
         reality,
For these (not for thyself) thou hast arrived.

Thou too surroundest all,
Embracing, carrying, welcoming all, thou too by
         pathways broad and new,
To the ideal tendest.

The measur'd faiths of other lands, the grandeurs
         of the past,
Are not for thee, but grandeurs of thine own,
Deific faiths and amplitudes, absorbing, compre-
         hending all,
All eligible to all.

All, all for immortality,
Love like the light silently wrapping all,
Nature's amelioration blessing all,
The blossoms, fruits of ages, orchards divine and
  certain,
Forms, objects, growths, humanities, to spiritual
  images ripening.

Give me, O God, to sing that thought,
Give me, give him or her I love, this quenchless
  faith,
In Thy ensemble, whatever else withheld, with-
  hold not from us,
Belief in plan of Thee enclosed in Time and Space,
Health, peace, salvation universal.

Is it a dream?
Nay but the lack of it the dream,
And failing it life's lore and wealth a dream,
And all the world a dream.

Walt Whitman

TO CAPTAIN DALE MABRY

*(The clothes were found burned from his body and the
flesh from his fingers, but the fingers still grasped the
wheel of the aircraft. — News Item.)*

At the portal of bright Valhalla
They bade a stranger stand.
"And where is your dented armor?
And where is your reeking brand?
Was it some mighty battle,
Where ye sloughed your body, then,

That ye stand at the close-tiled gateway
Of the Lodge of the Fighting Men?"

There came no word of answer
From the soul besmirched with smoke,
But, reining her rearing charger,
The fierce-eyed Valkyr spoke:
"Out of the whirling fury
Of the scarlet flames I come;
It was there that I found his spirit,
And I bring his spirit home!

"Over the dying Roma
The roaring fire-cloud swept
To the post in its blazing pathway;
To the post that his spirit kept;
I charge you bid him welcome,
Not for his sword-blade's steel,
But the charred and twisted handclasps
On the charred and twisted wheel!"

At the portal of bright Valhalla
The sentinel stands aside,
And cries his name to the chamber,
Where the souls of the brave abide;
Their blades have flashed from their scab-
        bards,
They have bidden a welcome high —
The men who died in their courage —
To the man who knew how to die.

                    Frederic F. Van de Water

INDEX OF AUTHORS